Dear Friend,

I am pleased to send you this copy of *Jesus and the End Times* by Dr. Ron Rhodes, founder and president of Reasoning from the Scriptures Ministries.

God's Word instructs us to be ready for Christ's return, especially since none of us know the day or hour. This very timely book from Dr. Rhodes invites you to take an in-depth look at what Jesus Himself taught about the last days during His time on earth. You'll discover Jesus' teaching on topics including the rapture, tribulation, second coming, judgment, millennial kingdom, and more. It's my prayer that it will strengthen you during these uncertain days as we eagerly wait *"for our blessed hope, the appearing of the glory of our great God and Savior Jesus Christ"* (Titus 2:13, ESV).

For 70 years, God has used the Billy Graham Evangelistic Association (BGEA) and friends like you to reach people all over the world with the Gospel. I'm so thankful for the ways He has worked—and for what He is continuing to do in the lives of men, women, and children today.

If you represent one of the lives the Lord has touched, we would love to hear from you. Your story has the power to impact the lives of so many others. May God richly bless you.

Sincerely,

D1316234

If you would like to k̲_____ ____ ____istry, please contact us:

IN THE U.S.:
Billy Graham Evangelistic Association
1 Billy Graham Parkway
Charlotte, NC 28201-0001
BillyGraham.org
info@bgea.org
Toll-free: 1-877-247-2426

IN CANADA:
Billy Graham Evangelistic
   Association of Canada
20 Hopewell Way NE
Calgary, AB T3J 5H5
BillyGraham.ca
Toll-free: 1-888-393-0003

A *Billy Graham Library Selection* designates materials that are appropriate for a well-rounded collection of quality Christian literature, including both classic and contemporary reading and reference materials.

This *Billy Graham Library Selection* special edition is published with permission from Harvest House Publishers.

Unless otherwise indicated, all Scripture quotations are taken from the Holy Bible, New Living Translation, ©1996, 2004, 2015 by Tyndale House Foundation. Used by permission of Tyndale House Publishers, Inc., Carol Stream, Illinois 60188. All rights reserved.

Verses marked ESV are from The ESV® Bible (the Holy Bible, English Standard Version®), ©2001 by Crossway, a publishing ministry of Good News Publishers. Used by permission. All rights reserved.

Verses marked AMP are taken from the Amplified® Bible, ©2015 by The Lockman Foundation. Used by permission. (www.Lockman.org)

Verses marked NKJV are taken from the New King James Version®. ©1982 by Thomas Nelson, Inc. Used by permission. All rights reserved.

Scripture text that appears in italics is the author's emphasis.

Cover photo ©Ig0rZh, bestdesign / Getty Images

Cover by Bryce Williamson, Eugene, OR

Jesus and the End Times
©2019 Ron Rhodes
Published by Harvest House Publishers
Eugene, Oregon 97408
www.harvesthousepublishers.com

Library of Congress Cataloging-in-Publication Data

Names: Rhodes, Ron, author.
Title: Jesus and the end times / Ron Rhodes.
Description: Eugene, Oregon : Harvest House Publishers, [2018] | Includes bibliographical references and index.
Identifiers: LCCN 2018023845 (print) | LCCN 2018039142 (ebook) | ISBN 9780736971720 (ebook) | ISBN 978073697173 (pbk.)
Subjects: LCSH: End of the world--Biblical teaching. | Jesus Christ--Biblical teaching. | Second Advent--Biblical teaching.
Classification: LCCBT877 (ebook) | LCCBT877 .R46 2018 (print) | DDC 202/ .3--dc23
LC record available at https://lccn.loc.gov/2018023845

ISBN-978-0-7369-7171-3 (pbk.)
ISBN-978-0-7369-7172-0 (eBook)
ISBN: 978-1-59328-650-7 (BGEA edition)

All rights reserved. No part of this publication may be reproduced, stored in a retrieval system, or transmitted in any form or by any means—electronic, mechanical, digital, photocopy, recording, or any other—except for brief quotations in printed reviews, without the prior permission of the publisher.

Printed in the United States of America
18 19 20 21 22 23 24 25 26 27 / BP-GL / 10 9 8 7 6 5 4 3 2 1

JESUS
AND THE
END TIMES

RON RHODES

HARVEST HOUSE PUBLISHERS
EUGENE, OREGON

This *Billy Graham Library Selection* special edition is published with
permission from Harvest House Publishers.

Acknowledgments

I wish to publicly acknowledge and thank the late Dr. John F. Walvoord, my primary prophecy mentor at Dallas Theological Seminary (DTS) in the 1980s. I also continue to appreciate Dr. J. Dwight Pentecost at DTS for his comprehensive courses on the prophetic books of Daniel and Revelation. The insightful teachings of Walvoord and Pentecost played a significant role in shaping my views on biblical prophecy.

I continue to be full of gratitude for my wife, Kerri, not only for the blessing she is in my life today, but also for the blessing she was during my seven years of graduate study at DTS. From the very beginning, she has faithfully stood by me and my work, and I could not have engaged in this life of ministry without her.

I remain eternally grateful to the Lord for blessing Kerri and me with two wonderful children—David and Kylie, both now grown—whose lives and Christian commitment are never-ending sources of inspiration. What an awesome family the Lord has given us.

Heartfelt appreciation goes to Bob Hawkins Jr. and the entire staff at Harvest House Publishers. Their professionalism and commitment to truth are shining examples among Christian publishers.

Finally—and most importantly—I am appreciative to the Lord Jesus Christ, whose teachings on prophecy are the focus of this book. *Thank You, Lord, for Your many blessings.*

Contents

Introduction:
Jesus and the End Times

When Jesus came to earth as the divine Messiah, He fulfilled the three primary offices of Prophet, Priest, and King. As Prophet, Jesus gave major discourses such as the Upper Room Discourse (John 14–16), the Olivet Discourse, which contains many prophetic teachings (Matthew 24–25), and the Sermon on the Mount (Matthew 5–7). He also spoke as a prophet on many occasions when addressing the kingdom of God (also called the kingdom of heaven).

Unlike human prophets, who were simply God's spokesmen, Jesus as Prophet is intrinsically omniscient, or all-knowing. He knows the future just as comprehensively as He knows the past. In fact, all who came into close contact with Jesus seemed to sense that He was omniscient or all-knowing. The apostle John said of Jesus, "No one needed to tell him about human nature, for he knew what was in each person's heart" (John 2:25). Jesus's disciples said, "Now we understand that you know everything, and there's no need to question you" (16:30). After His resurrection from the dead, when Jesus asked Peter for the third time if Peter loved Him, Peter responded, "Lord, you know everything" (21:17).

Bible scholar Thomas Schultz provides us with an excellent summary of biblical evidences for Christ's omniscience:

First, He knows the inward thoughts and memories of man, an ability peculiar to God (1 Kings 8:39; Jeremiah 17:9-16). He saw the evil in the hearts of the scribes (Matthew 9:4); He knew beforehand those who would reject Him (John 6:64) and those who would follow Him (John 10:14). He could read the hearts of every man and woman (Mark 2:8; John 1:48; 2:24-25; 4:16-19; Acts 1:24; 1 Corinthians 4:5; Revelation 2:18-23). A mere human can no more than make an intelligent guess as to what is in the hearts and minds of others.

Second, Christ has a knowledge of other facts beyond the possible comprehension of any man. He knew just where the fish were in the water (Luke 5:4,6; John 21:6-11), and He knew just which fish contained the coin in its mouth (Matthew 17:27). He knew future events (John 11:11; 18:4), details that would be encountered (Matthew 21:2-4), and He knew that Lazarus had died (John 11:14).

Third, He possessed an inner knowledge of the God-head showing the closest possible communion with God as well as perfect knowledge. He knows the Father as the Father knows Him (Matthew 11:27; John 7:29; 8:55; 10:15; 17:25).

The fourth and consummating teaching of Scripture along this line is that Christ knows all things (John 16:30; 21:17), and that in Him are hidden all the treasures of wisdom and knowledge (Colossians 2:3).[1]

An additional evidence for Christ's omniscience is that He hears and answers the prayers of His people all over the world (Acts 7:59; 9:6; 1 Corinthians 1:1-2; 2 Corinthians 12:8-9; Revelation 22:20). "When Jesus claimed for himself the prerogative to hear and to answer the prayers of his disciples," New Testament scholar Robert Reymond suggests, "he was making an implicit claim to the possession of omniscience. One who can hear the innumerable prayers of his disciples, offered to him night and day, day in and day out throughout the centuries, keep each request infallibly related to its petitioner, and answer them in accordance with the divine mind and will would need himself to be omniscient."[2] That's a pretty amazing insight.

Of course, the point I am building up to is that Jesus—as omniscient deity—comprehensively knows the future. This means that His prophetic teachings about the future are trustworthy. He knows what He's talking about. Count on it.

Christ Spoke Through the Old Testament Prophets

In 1 Peter 1:10-11, the apostle Peter spoke of the prophets and their words about salvation in Christ: "This salvation was something even the prophets wanted to know more about when they prophesied about this gracious salvation prepared for you. They wondered what time or situation the Spirit of Christ within them was talking about when he told them in advance about Christ's suffering and his great glory afterward."

Scholars have debated what may be meant by the phrase "Spirit of Christ." Grammatically, the phrase may refer either to Christ Himself (as the Spirit *of* Christ) or to the Holy Spirit (as the Spirit *from* Christ). The form of the word in the original Greek text is the same in either case (*Christou*).[3]

A number of scholars have concluded that it was indeed Christ's spirit who was at work in the prophets.[4] Based on this verse, Clement of Alexandria suggested that Jesus was "the Prophet of prophets, and Lord of all the prophetical spirit."[5]

Along these same lines, theologian Millard Erickson summarizes:

> Christ's revealing work covers a wide span of time and forms. He first functioned in a revelatory fashion even before his incarnation. As the Logos, he is the light which has enlightened everyone coming into the world; thus, in a sense all truth has come from and through him (John

1:9). There are indications that Christ himself was at work in the revelations which came through the prophets who bore a message about him…(1 Peter 1:11). Although not personally incarnate, Christ was already making the truth known."[6]

Bible scholar R.C.H. Lenski in like manner commented that in 1 Peter 1:11, "the deity and the pre-existence of Christ are involved: Christ's Spirit testified in advance about Christ's sufferings and glories, that is, when as the incarnate Logos he would suffer in his humiliation and after that be crowned with glories in his exaltation."[7]

I am convinced this is the correct view. But for those who are not sure, one further consideration bears mentioning. Even if the phrase "Spirit of Christ" refers not to Christ's spirit but to the Holy Spirit, we must acknowledge that the Holy Spirit as the "Spirit of Christ" was doing Christ's bidding in the prophets—*providing prophetic truth on Christ's behalf.* In John 16:14-15, Jesus affirmed of the Holy Spirit, "He will bring me glory by telling you whatever he receives from me…The Spirit will tell you whatever he receives from me."

Christ's Prophetic Teachings in the Gospels

Christ spoke quite a bit about biblical prophecy in the New Testament Gospels. Much of it is found in His Olivet Discourse, so named because He was sitting on the Mount of Olives when He delivered the discourse (Matthew 24–25). The disciples had come to Him to inquire, "What sign will signal your return and the end of the world?" (24:3). The entire Olivet Discourse should be viewed as His response to this question.

Highlights of Jesus's teaching in this discourse include His prediction of the signs of the end of the age—including the appearance of false Christs, wars, earthquakes, famines, the profaning of the Jewish temple, various cosmic disturbances, and the sign of His coming (Matthew 24:4-31). He also spoke of how the end times will be much like the days of Noah:

> In those days before the flood, the people were enjoying banquets and parties and weddings right up to the time Noah entered his boat. People didn't realize what was going to happen until the flood came and swept them all away. That is the way it will be when the Son of Man comes (Matthew 24:38-39).

Jesus consistently stressed the importance of being ready for when He returns (Matthew 24:32-35,45-51; 25:1-13,14-30). He also prophesied about the judgment of the nations that will transpire immediately following His second coming (25:31-46). This judgment will determine who will be permitted to enter into Christ's millennial kingdom (more on all this later in the book).

Of course, Jesus set forth other prophetic teachings aside from those found in the Olivet Discourse. He affirmed, for example, that He would one day come for His followers at the rapture and bring them back with Him to heaven (John 14:1-3). In this book we will see that prophecy was a major component of the teachings of Christ throughout His three-year ministry. We would therefore be wise to pay close attention to His prophetic teachings.

The Course of the Present Age

Jesus also spoke prophetically about the course of the present age. The theological backdrop to this is that the Davidic kingdom (2 Samuel 7:8-14) had been offered to the Jewish people by the divine Messiah, Jesus Christ (Matthew 11–12). However, the Jewish leaders not only rejected Jesus, but claimed His miracles were performed not in the power of the Holy Spirit but in the power of Satan, the *un*holy spirit. This constituted a definitive and flagrant turning away from Jesus as the Jewish Messiah. The apostle Paul informed us that this is why a judicial blindness and hardening was inflicted upon Israel as a judgment from God—a blindness and hardening that will not be removed until the end times (Romans 11:25).

God's kingdom program was thereby altered, with a delay in the coming of the offered kingdom. In fact, it will be delayed until the future 1,000-year millennial kingdom, which will follow the second coming of Christ.

That being the case, Jesus, in Matthew 13, provided insights to His followers as to what the course of the present age would be like up till the time of His second coming. Jesus provided these insights in the form of parables.

The word *parable* means "a placing alongside of" for the purpose of comparison. A parable is a teaching tool. Jesus often told a story from real life—involving, for example, a woman who lost a coin, or a shepherd watching over sheep, or a worker in a vineyard—and used that story to illustrate some particular spiritual truth. By taking such a story and "placing it alongside" a spiritual truth, Jesus helped His followers to understand His spiritual teachings more clearly. As an example, His story of the good shepherd helps us to understand that Jesus watches over us and guides us, just as a shepherd watches over and guides sheep.

Some of Jesus's parables provide us insights on the course of the present age. I will address these prophetic parables in detail in chapter 6. To whet your appetite, however, the parable of the sower teaches that this age will be characterized by the sowing of the gospel seed onto different kinds of soil (Matthew 13:1-23). This reveals that there will be various kinds of responses to the gospel, including opposition to the gospel from the world, the flesh, and the devil.

The parable of the tares indicates that the true sowing of the gospel seed will be imitated by a false counter-sowing (Matthew 13:24-30). Only a judgment following the future tribulation period will separate the "wheat" (true believers) from the "weeds" (unbelievers, or false believers).

The parable of the mustard seed indicates that God's spiritual kingdom would have an almost imperceptible beginning—hardly even noticeable. But just as a small mustard seed can produce a large plant (it can grow up past 15 feet high), so God's spiritual kingdom would start small but grow to be very large in the world by the time of the second coming (Matthew 13:31-32).

The parable of the hidden treasure has been interpreted in various ways by biblical scholars (Matthew 13:44). Many believe Jesus was pointing to the incredible value of the true kingdom of heaven, as opposed to counterfeit belief systems (such as the cults and false religions that are so prominent in our day). Those who truly see the kingdom's importance will do anything within their power to possess it. They will allow nothing to stand in their way.

In the parable of the net (Matthew 13:47-50), Jesus indicated that up until the second coming, when judgment will take place, there will be both genuine Christians and phony (professing) Christians that coexist within the kingdom. At the end of the age, there will be a separation of the righteous from the unrighteous, just as good fish are separated from bad fish caught in a net. The righteous (that is, true believers) will be invited into Christ's kingdom, while the unrighteous (professing believers who are actually unbelievers) will be excluded from His kingdom and sent to a place of suffering (see Matthew 25:31-46).

We conclude from these (and other) parables that Jesus's prophetic teachings address not only the more distant end times, but also describe the religious landscape in the many centuries that precede the end times. Jesus, as God, was omnisciently able to see the entire panoramic sweep of human history, right up till the end.

The Book of Revelation—a Revelation from Jesus Christ

In Revelation 1:1-2 we read, "This is a revelation from Jesus Christ, which God gave him to show his servants the events that must soon take place. He sent an angel to present this revelation to his servant John, who faithfully reported everything he saw." The phrase "revelation *from* Jesus Christ" can also be translated "revelation *of* Jesus Christ." It is likely that both senses are intended in this verse. The book of Revelation contains prophetic truth that comes *from* Jesus Christ and is also *about* Jesus Christ.

Notice that "God gave" this revelation to Jesus Christ (Revelation 1:1). This simply means that God the Father gave this revelation to God the Son. The Father is the source. Jesus is the revealer. This reminds us of John 12:49, where Jesus affirmed, "I don't speak on my own authority. The Father who sent me has commanded me what to say and how to say it."

Jesus, in the book of Revelation, reveals "events that must soon take place" (Revelation 1:1). This should not be taken to mean that the events described in Revelation would all take place within a few years of the time John saw them. John recorded Revelation in the Greek language, and the Greek word translated "soon" can mean "quickly," "swiftly," "speedily," and "at a rapid rate" (see Luke 18:8). In Revelation 1:1, the term indicates that when the predicted events first start to occur in the end times, they will then progress rapidly.

I have written separately about the book of Revelation (see *40 Days Through Revelation*, published by Harvest House Publishers). Here in this book, we will see that Christ's prophetic teachings in Revelation coincide quite nicely with His prophetic teachings in the four Gospels, especially the Olivet Discourse.

Be Accurate Observers of the End Times

In view of the importance Christ gave to prophetic truths, we should all seek to be accurate observers of the times. We are motivated to do this when we consider Jesus's words in Matthew 16:1-3:

> One day the Pharisees and Sadducees came to test Jesus, demanding that he show them a miraculous sign from heaven to prove his authority.
>
> He replied, "You know the saying, 'Red sky at night means fair weather tomorrow; red sky in the morning means foul weather all day.' You know how to interpret the weather signs in the sky, but you don't know how to interpret the signs of the times!"

What a rebuke! These guys—the religious elite of the time—were supposed to know the teachings of the prophets, and yet they were completely unable to properly discern the times. The Pharisees and Sadducees had been surrounded by spiritual signs of Jesus's identity and they had missed them all. They were blinded to the reality that the Messiah was with them. Jesus's miracles pointed to His divine identity just as surely as dark clouds signal rain. The Old Testament prophesied about the Messiah's miracles—the blind will see, the deaf will hear, and the lame will walk (Isaiah 35:5-6). The Pharisees and Sadducees—experts in the Old Testament—should have realized that Jesus fulfilled these messianic verses. After all, blind people were given sight, deaf people were enabled to hear, and lame people could now walk. But in their blindness and hardened hearts, these religious leaders could not "interpret the signs of the times."

Let's not follow their example. Let's seek to understand the prophetic signs of the times relating to end-time events leading up to Christ's second coming and beyond.

Jesus also urged, "Now learn a lesson from the fig tree. When its branches bud and its leaves begin to sprout, you know that summer is near. In the same way, when you see all these things, you can know his return is very near, right at the door" (Matthew 24:32-33). In this passage, Jesus indicated that God has revealed certain things in prophecy that ought to cause people who know the Bible to understand that a fulfillment of prophecy is taking place—or perhaps the stage is being set for a prophecy to eventually be fulfilled. Jesus was thus informing His followers to be accurate observers of the times so that they could take note when biblical prophecies were being fulfilled (see also Luke 21:25-28). I encourage you to reflect on this often as we proceed through the book. (I'll provide more details on the parable of the fig tree in chapter 4.)

> *Lord, by the power of Your Spirit, please enable us to understand the prophetic teachings of our blessed Prophet, Priest, and King, Jesus Christ. As we proceed, please excite us with Your Word and instill a sense of awe for the person of our Lord Jesus Christ. We thank You in Jesus's name. Amen.*

1

The Rapture

The rapture is a glorious event in which Christ will descend from heaven, the dead in Christ will be resurrected, and living Christians will be instantly translated into their glorified bodies. Both groups will be caught up to meet Christ in the air and taken back to heaven (1 Thessalonians 4:13-17; John 14:1-3; 1 Corinthians 15:51-54). This means one generation of Christians will never pass through death's door.

The rapture will be an instantaneous event—"in a moment, in the blink of an eye" (1 Corinthians 15:52). One moment Christians will be on earth in their mortal bodies, and the next moment they will meet Christ in the clouds, instantly transformed into their glorified bodies.

The apostle Paul calls this event a "wonderful secret":

Let me reveal to you a wonderful secret. We will not all die, but we will all be transformed! It will happen in a moment, in the blink of an eye, when the last trumpet is blown. For when the trumpet sounds, those who have died will be raised to live forever. And we who are living will also be transformed. For our dying bodies must be transformed into bodies that will never die; our mortal bodies must be transformed into immortal bodies.

Then, when our dying bodies have been transformed into bodies that will never die, this Scripture will be fulfilled: "Death is swallowed up in victory. O death, where is your victory? O death, where is your sting?" (1 Corinthians 15:51-55).

The Greek word translated "secret" in this passage means "mystery." A mystery, in the biblical sense, is a truth that cannot be discerned merely by human investigation but requires special revelation from God. Generally, this word refers to a truth that was unknown to people living in Old Testament times but is now revealed to us by God (Matthew 13:17; Colossians 1:26). The doctrine of the resurrection was known in Old Testament times (Job 19:25-27; Psalm 49:15; Isaiah 26:19; Daniel 12:2), but the doctrine of the rapture was not revealed until New Testament times (1 Thessalonians 4:13-17; 1 Corinthians 15:50-52; Revelation 3:10). Jesus Himself spoke about the rapture several times in His prophetic teachings.

Jesus Promises to Rapture Us

John 14–16 contains Jesus's Upper Room Discourse. In John 14:1-3, Jesus gives us an amazing prophecy of the rapture:

> Don't let your hearts be troubled. Trust in God, and trust also in me. There is more than enough room in my Father's home. If this were not so, would I have told you that I am going to prepare a place for you? When everything is ready, I will come and get you, so that you will always be with me where I am.

My former prophecy mentor at Dallas Theological Seminary, John F. Walvoord, had a great insight on this passage of Scripture:

> These verses are the Bible's first revelation of the rapture, in

which Christ will come back to take His own to heaven. He exhorted the disciples not to be troubled. Since they trusted the Father, they also should trust Christ, whose power was demonstrated in His many miracles. Having referred to Himself as the Source of peace, Jesus spoke of His coming to take them to heaven. They need not be anxious about His leaving because later He would return for them.[1]

Regardless of what happens in this world, we do not need to be troubled. Why not? Because we know the Prince of Peace, Jesus Christ. He is the source of our peace, and the peace He gives does not depend on circumstances: "I am leaving you with a gift—peace of mind and heart. And the peace I give is a gift the world cannot give. So don't be troubled or afraid" (John 14:27). We need not worry. We need not fear. This is especially so because we know that Christ is coming for us at the rapture. We may not know precisely *when* Christ is coming for us, but the *fact* that He is coming for us can be a huge boost to our emotions.

The Bride/Bridegroom Metaphor

Scripture portrays Christ as the Bridegroom (John 3:29) and the church as His bride (Revelation 19:7). The backdrop to this imagery is rooted in Hebrew weddings, which had three phases. First, the marriage betrothal—a binding commitment often arranged a year or more prior to marriage—was legally consummated by the parents of the bride and groom, after which the groom went to prepare a place to live in his father's house. Next, the bridegroom came to claim his bride. Finally, there was a wedding and marriage supper, which could last several days. All three of these phases are seen in Christ's relationship to the church, the bride of Christ, and are particularly relevant to our understanding of Christ's teaching on the rapture in John 14:1-3.

1. As individuals living during the church age come to salvation, under the Father's loving and sovereign hand, they become a part of the bride of Christ (the church) (see John 6:44,65). Meanwhile, Christ, the Bridegroom, is in heaven, preparing a place for the bride of Christ to live in His Father's house (John 14:2).

2. The Bridegroom (Jesus Christ) will one day come to claim His bride (at the rapture) and take her to heaven, where He has prepared a place for her (John 14:1-3). The actual marriage will take place in heaven prior to the second coming (Revelation 19:6-16).

3. The marriage supper of the Lamb will follow the second coming, prior to Christ's setting up of the millennial kingdom (see Daniel 12:11; compare with Matthew 22:1-14; 25:1-13).

We can see other parallels as well. Just as Jewish grooms paid a purchase price to establish the marriage covenant, so Jesus paid a purchase price for the church (1 Corinthians 6:19-20). Also, just as a Jewish bride was declared sanctified or set apart in waiting for her groom, so the church is declared sanctified and set apart for Christ the Bridegroom (Ephesians 5:25-27; 1 Corinthians 1:2; 6:11; Hebrews 10:10; 13:12). And just as a Jewish bride was unaware of the exact time her groom would come for her, so the church is unaware of the exact time Jesus the Bridegroom will come at the rapture, though it is an imminent event. It could happen at any time.

This idea of imminence supports a pretribulational rapture. After all, if the rapture takes place after the tribulation, the rapture would be preceded by seven years of prophetic signs. We would therefore be able to predict when the Bridegroom would come for His bride. The bride/Bridegroom metaphor seems much more in keeping with a pretribulational rapture, with the bride (the church) not knowing precisely when the Bridegroom will come for her.

Parallels Between Jesus and Paul

It is interesting to see how similar Jesus's teachings on the rapture are to those of the apostle Paul. One need only compare Jesus's prophetic words in John 14:1-3 with Paul's prophetic words in 1 Thessalonians 4:13-18 to see noticeable parallels:

- John 14:3 depicts Jesus as coming to the earth ("I will come"), which obviously involves a descent from the heavenly realm. Likewise, in 1 Thessalonians 4:16, Paul said Christ "will come down from heaven."

- In John 14:3 Jesus said to believers: "I...will take you to myself" (ESV). In 1 Thessalonians 4:17, Paul revealed that believers will be "caught up" to meet Christ in the air.

- In John 14:3 Jesus revealed that believers will be with Him ("you will always be with me where I am"). In 1 Thessalonians 4:17, Paul affirmed that believers "will be with the Lord forever."

- In John 14:1 Jesus revealed that the purpose of this revelation about the rapture is so that the hearts of Christ's followers would not be troubled. Likewise, in 1 Thessalonians 4:13,18, Paul revealed that the purpose of this revelation about the rapture was to minimize grief and bring encouragement.

Of course, it is not surprising that there are such similarities between Jesus's and Paul's teachings. After all, Jesus Himself affirmed that Paul was "my chosen instrument" who will speak "my message" (Acts 9:15). This means that Paul's words about the rapture were part of Christ's message.

Christ Is the Architect and Builder of Our Eternal Home

Prophetic Scripture reveals that Jesus Himself is the Architect and Builder of our eternal home, to which He will take us immediately following the rapture. He told His followers, "I am going to prepare a place for you" (John 14:2). I love pondering this verse. Sometimes when I go outside at night, I look up and see thousands of stars illuminating the sky. It boggles the mind to ponder that the same Christ who created the entire stellar universe (John 1:3; Colossians 1:16) is the One who is building a place for us in the Father's house (John 14:1-3).

Let's camp here for a moment. Consider the sheer magnitude of the stellar universe. Astronomers tell us that only about 4,000 stars are visible to the unaided human eye. Yet astronomers—using powerful telescopes—have discovered that there are more than 10 million billion billion stars in the known universe. And truth be told—who knows how many stars exist beyond the reach of our finite telescopes? The likelihood is that our universe is far more immense than our finite instruments could even begin to detect.[2]

The grandeur of the universe is evident not only in the number of stars, but also in their incredible distances from each other. Allow me to use an illustration. A ray of light travels at 186,000 miles per second. It would take that ray of light 2 minutes and 18 seconds to reach Venus because it's 26 million miles away. It would take four-and-one-half minutes for that ray to reach planet Mercury because it's 50 million miles away. The ray would take 35 minutes to reach Jupiter because it's 367 million miles away. Saturn would take an hour and 11 seconds because it's 790 million miles away. Pluto would take much longer because it's 2.7 billion miles away. Even then, we still haven't left our solar system.

The North Star is an incredible 400 hundred billion miles away. That sounds immense, but when compared to the size of the known universe, it's a relatively short distance. There's a star named Betelgeuse that is a phenomenal 880 quadrillion miles from us and has a diameter of 250 million miles. The diameter of this gargantuan star is greater than the earth's orbit around the sun. *Mind-blowing!*

As staggering as all this sounds, the entire universe, in all of its glory, was created through the agency of Jesus Christ: "Through him

[Christ] God created everything in the heavenly realms and on earth. He made the things we can see and the things we can't see—such as thrones, kingdoms, rulers, and authorities in the unseen world. Everything was created through him and for him" (Colossians 1:16). John 1:3 says of Christ, "God created everything through him, and nothing was created except through him."

Whether one is contemplating the incredible glory of the stars above, or fixing one's eyes upon beautiful sights on earth, none can deny that Jesus has amazing creative abilities. Anne Graham Lotz offers this inspiring insight about God the Son's creative abilities:

> Who created all the earthly beauty we have grown to love…the majestic snowcapped peaks of the Alps, the rushing mountain streams, the brilliantly colored fall leaves, the carpets of wildflowers, the glistening fin of a fish as it leaps out of a sparkling sea, the graceful gliding of a swan across the lake, the lilting notes of a canary's song, the whir of a hummingbird's wings, the shimmer of the dew on the grass in early morning…This is the same Creator who has prepared our heavenly home for us! If God could make the heavens and earth as beautiful as we think they are today— which includes thousands of years of wear and tear, corruption and pollution, sin and selfishness—can you imagine what the new heaven and the new earth will look like? It will be much more glorious than any eyes have seen, any ears have heard, or any minds have ever conceived.[3]

Revelation 21–22 reveals that the place Christ is now creating for us is a heavenly city called "the New Jerusalem." In this city, God will live directly with redeemed humankind—face to face (Revelation 21:3; compare with Leviticus 26:11-12; Deuteronomy 12:5). Here at last we find unfettered companionship between the Creator and His creation. And God "will wipe every tear from their eyes, and there will be no more death or sorrow or crying or pain.

All these things are gone forever" (Revelation 21:4). There will be no more disease, no more weakness, no more decay, no more coffins, no more funerals, and no more graves. There will be no reason for tears. Life in the eternal city will be painless, tearless, and deathless.

This is the place Jesus was referring to when He told His followers, "I am going to prepare a place for you" (John 14:2). Immediately following the rapture—when the dead in Christ are raised, living believers are instantly transformed into their glorified bodies, and we all meet the Lord in the air—we'll all go straight to this glorious heavenly city that Christ has prepared for us. How awesome it will be!

Jesus on the Timing of the Rapture

Jesus revealed in the book of Revelation that the rapture of the church will take place prior to the beginning of the tribulation—a seven-year period of God's judgment upon the world that precedes the second coming. In Revelation 3:10, Jesus makes this promise to the church at Philadelphia: "Because you have kept my word about patient endurance, I will keep you from the hour of trial that is coming on the whole world, to try those who dwell on the earth" (ESV). While the seven churches in Revelation 2 and 3 were historical churches in Asia Minor, many scholars believe these churches may also point in a secondary way to churches in the succeeding centuries of church history. If this is correct, then Revelation 3:10 may have application to the future rapture. We know for a fact that Jesus's statement to the church at Philadelphia was not intended to be limited to that church alone. After all, in the same passage, Jesus said, "Anyone with ears to hear must listen to the Spirit and understand what he is saying *to the churches*" (verse 13).

That being the case, let's unpack this verse a bit. Notice that there is a definite article ("the") before the phrase "hour of trial" in Revelation 3:10 ("*the* hour of trial") (ESV). In the English language, definite articles do not hold too much significance. But in the Greek language they are very important. Among other things, definite articles can indicate specificity. In Revelation 3:10, the definite article points to a specific and distinctive time period, not just any "hour of trial." There is good reason to believe it is a reference to the future tribulation period, which will be a seven-year "hour of trial" (ESV). This period of trial—the tribulation—is described in detail in Revelation 4–18. It is from this period of trial that the church is to be exempted.

I don't want to make too fine a point of it, but it's critical that you not miss Jesus's declaration that the church is to be kept *from the time period itself.* If the Lord meant to communicate that He would preserve church believers *through* this time of testing, He would not have said, "I will keep you *from* the hour of trial."

The Greek preposition (*ek*), translated "from" in this verse ("I will keep you *from* the hour of trial"), carries the idea of *separation* from something. This means that believers will be kept from the hour of testing in the sense that they will be completely separated from it by being raptured before the period begins (1 Thessalonians 1:10; 5:9).

Renald Showers, in his helpful book *Maranatha: Our Lord, Come!,* suggests that "the language in Jesus's reference to this future period of worldwide testing implied that it was well-known to the church saints. It was well-known because both Old and New Testament Scriptures, written years before Revelation, foretold this unique, future period of testing or Tribulation, which would take place prior to the coming of the Messiah to rule the world in the Messianic Age or Millennium (Isa. 2:10-21; Dan. 12:1; Zeph. 1:14-18; Mt. 24:4-31)."[4]

Of course, this verse promises that *only church-age saints* will be kept out of this hour of trial that will come upon the entire earth. Those who become believers during the hour of trial itself—whom we might call tribulation saints—will go through the remainder of the tribulation. This is an important observation, as noted by prophecy expert Arnold Fruchtenbaum in his book *The Footsteps of the Messiah*:

> Throughout the Tribulation, saints are being killed on a massive scale (Rev. 6:9–11; 11:7; 12:11; 13:7, 15; 14:13; 17:6; 18:24). If these saints are Church saints, they are not being kept safe and Revelation 3:10 is meaningless. Only if Church saints and Tribulation saints are kept distinct does the promise of Revelation 3:10 make any sense.[5]

One may wonder how people will become believers during the tribulation period. Perhaps they become convinced of the truth of Christianity after witnessing millions of Christians supernaturally vanish off the planet at the rapture. Or perhaps they will become believers as a result of the ministry of the 144,000 Jewish evangelists introduced in Revelation 7 (who themselves come to faith in Christ sometime after the rapture). Or maybe they will become believers as a result of the miraculous ministry of the two witnesses of Revelation 11, prophets who apparently will have the same kinds of powers as Moses and Elijah. As well, Christian literature will be left behind after the rapture, and many may come to faith after reading such books.

What About Jesus's Prophecy in Matthew 24:40-41?

Some Christians appeal to Jesus's prophecy in Matthew 24:40-41 and claim that Jesus taught the rapture will occur following the tribulation period, not before it. In this passage, Jesus stated, "Two men will be working together in the field; one will be taken, the other left. Two women will be grinding flour at the mill; one will be taken, the other left." It is reasoned that because this passage occurs in a second-coming context, it must refer to a posttribulational rapture.

The problem with this view is that a comparison of this passage to a key cross-reference shows that those who are taken are removed not in the rapture, but are *taken away in judgment*, to be punished. In Luke 17:35-37, Jesus states, "There will be two women grinding together. One will be taken and the other left. And they said to him, 'Where, Lord?' He said to them, 'Where the corpse is, there the vultures will gather" (ESV). Those who are "taken" become corpses that feed the vultures. This type of language was often used among the Jews as a metaphor for judgment (see Ezekiel 28:26; 32:4-6; 39:17-20; 1 Samuel 17:44; Psalm 79:2). Hence, the passage does not refer to being taken in the rapture, but rather, being taken away in judgment. Those who are "left" are the righteous who will enter into Christ's millennial kingdom on earth (see Matthew 25:31-46).

I will address Jesus's teachings on judgment and the millennial kingdom later in the book. In this next chapter, we will zero in on Jesus's teachings about the tribulation period, which follows the rapture.

2

The Tribulation Period, Part 1

The word *tribulation*, in the original Greek text of the New Testament, has a number of shades of meaning. I'm talking about the word *thlipsis*, which means "to press" (as grapes), "to press together," "to press hard upon," and typically refers to times of oppression, affliction, and distress. It can be translated variously as "tribulation," "affliction," "anguish," "persecution," "trouble," and "burden."

In the New Testament, the word is used in a variety of contexts. For example, it is used in relation to those hard pressed by the calamities of war (Matthew 24:21), as well as a woman giving birth to a child (John 16:21). It is used of those pressed by severe poverty and lack (Philippians 4:14), as well as general oppressive anxiety and burden of heart (2 Corinthians 2:4). The word is even used to speak of the severe afflictions of Jesus Christ (Colossians 1:24).

It is critical that we distinguish between the general tribulation that all Christians experience in the world and the specific period of tribulation that will take place during the end times. All Christians may expect a certain amount of general tribulation in their lives. Jesus Himself said to the disciples, "Here on earth you will have many trials and sorrows" (John 16:33). Paul and Barnabas warned that "we must suffer many hardships to enter the Kingdom of God" (Acts 14:22).

Scripture also teaches, however, that there will be a definite period of tribulation at the end of the age (Matthew 24:29-35). It will be of such severity that no period in history—past or future—will equal it (Matthew 24:21). Jesus affirmed that this period will be shortened for the elects' sake (Matthew 24:22), as no flesh could survive if it were to go on indefinitely. This period of tribulation is called "a time of trouble for my people Israel" (Jeremiah 30:7), for it is a judgment on Messiah-rejecting Israel (Daniel 12:1-4). During this time, the nations of the world will also be judged for their sin and rejection of Christ (Isaiah 26:21; Revelation 6:15-17). The period is described as being seven years in length (Daniel 9:24,27), and it will be so bad that people will want to hide and even die (Revelation 6:16).

The tribulation period will be characterized by wrath (Zephaniah 1:15,18), judgment (Revelation 14:7), indignation (Isaiah 26:20-21), trial (Revelation 3:10), trouble (Jeremiah 30:7), destruction (Joel 1:15), darkness (Amos 5:18), desolation (Daniel 9:27), overturning (Isaiah 24:1-4), and punishment (Isaiah 24:20-21). It will be the most vexing and agonizing time in human history.

This tribulation will be global. Revelation 3:10 describes it as "the great time of testing that will *come upon the whole world* to test those who belong to this world." Isaiah likewise tells us, "Look! The LORD is about to destroy the earth and make it a vast wasteland. He devastates the surface of the earth and scatters the people" (Isaiah 24:1). He warns, "Terror and traps and snares will be your lot, you people of the earth" (verse 17). Nowhere on earth will be safe.

As for the source of the tribulation, Scripture affirms that this will be a period of both divine wrath and satanic wrath—especially divine wrath. The tribulation is a "day of the LORD's anger" (Zephaniah 1:18). The earth will experience "the wrath of the Lamb" (Revelation 6:16-17). "The LORD is about to destroy the earth" (Isaiah 24:1) "The LORD is coming from heaven to punish the people of the earth for their sins" (Isaiah 26:21). Satan's wrath is evident in Revelation 12:4,13,17.

God has several purposes for the tribulation period. First, it will conclude what is called "the period of the Gentiles"—the extended time of Gentile domination over Jerusalem (Luke 21:24). Second, the tribulation will bring judgment against the Christ-rejecting nations of the world. And third, the tribulation will prepare for the restoration and the regathering of Israel in the millennial kingdom of Christ, which will follow His second coming. Hence, even though the tribulation period is frightening, it is a necessary component in the unfolding of God's prophetic plan.

In what follows I'll demonstrate some notable parallels between Jesus's prophetic teachings in the Olivet Discourse and those found in the book of Revelation. Of course, we would expect there to be parallels in view of the fact that the prophetic teachings in the book of Revelation were given to John by Jesus Himself. We read in Revelation 1:1-2, "This is a revelation from Jesus Christ, which God gave him to show his servants the events that must soon take place. He sent an angel to present this revelation to his servant John, who faithfully reported everything he saw." Both sets of prophetic revelation have the same ultimate source—*Jesus!*

False Christs and the Antichrist

We begin with the recognition that Jesus warned about the rise of false Christs during the tribulation period: "Don't let anyone mislead you, for many will come in my name, claiming, 'I am the Messiah.' They will deceive many" (Matthew 24:4-5; see also 2 Corinthians 11:4). The danger, of course, is that a counterfeit Jesus who preaches a counterfeit gospel yields a counterfeit salvation (see Galatians 1:8). There are no exceptions to this maxim. Even in our own day, we witness an unprecedented rise in false Christs and self-constituted messiahs affiliated with the kingdom of the cults and the occult. This will no doubt continue to escalate as we move further into the end times.

Christ's warning about false Christs in the Olivet Discourse seems parallel to what we read about the first seal judgment, where John spoke of the rise of the antichrist—the ultimate false Christ: "I looked up and saw a white horse standing there. Its rider carried a bow, and a crown was placed on his head. He rode out to win many battles and gain the victory" (Revelation 6:1-2).

Notice that the first four seal judgments are also known as the four horsemen of the apocalypse. The first horse is white. Some have speculated that perhaps the rider of the white horse may be Jesus because He is seen to ride a white horse in Revelation 19:11 at the second coming. However, the contexts are entirely different. In Revelation 19, Christ returns to the earth as a conqueror on a horse at the end of the tribulation. By contrast, Revelation 6 deals with a rider on a horse at the beginning of the tribulation. He is joined by three other horses and their riders, and they are all associated with the seal judgments, all unleashed by Christ Himself. Most scholars believe the rider of the white horse in Revelation 6:2 is none other than the antichrist (Daniel 9:26). The crown suggests that the individual is a ruler. The bow without an arrow signifies that the antichrist's world government will initially be established without warfare. His government will seem to begin with a time of peace, but that peace will be short-lived, for destruction will surely follow (see 1 Thessalonians 5:3).

Wars and Threats of Wars

In the Olivet Discourse, Jesus prophesied, "You will hear of wars and threats of wars...Nation will go to war against nation, and kingdom against kingdom" (Matthew 24:6-7). In the second seal judgment in the book of Revelation—also known as the second horseman of the apocalypse—we read that "another horse appeared, a red one. Its rider was given a mighty sword and the authority to take peace from the earth. And there was war and slaughter everywhere" (Revelation 6:3-4). The "war and slaughter everywhere" seems parallel to "kingdom against kingdom" around the world (Matthew 24:7).

Of course, red is a color that represents bloodshed, killing with the sword, and war. The rider of the second horseman of the apocalypse carries a "mighty" sword, indicating that major weaponry will be unleashed during the tribulation, yielding much blood. Peace will be taken from the entire earth.

The End Is Not Yet

After prophesying "wars and threats of wars," Jesus said, "These things must take place, but the end won't follow immediately" (Matthew 24:6). Recall that the second seal judgment removes peace from the earth, and there will be "war and slaughter everywhere" (Revelation 6:3-4). Note, however, that this judgment will take place during the first half of the tribulation period. Wars will continue throughout the rest of the tribulation, culminating in Armageddon—that final series of battles that immediately precedes Christ's second coming. This is why Jesus prophesied that "the end won't follow immediately" when wars break out during the early part of the tribulation period.

Famines and Earthquakes

In the Olivet Discourse, Jesus prophesied, "There will be famines and earthquakes in many parts of the world" (Matthew 24:7). In the third seal judgment in the book of Revelation—also known as the third horseman of the apocalypse—we read, "'Come!' I looked up and saw a black horse, and its rider was holding a pair of scales in his hand. And I heard a voice from among the four living beings say, 'A loaf of wheat bread or three loaves of barley will cost a day's pay. And don't waste the olive oil and wine'" (Revelation 6:5-6).

The pair of scales in the rider's hand apparently symbolizes famine (with subsequent death) as prices for wheat and barley soar extravagantly high, requiring a full day's wages just to buy a few meals (see Lamentations 5:8-10). Such a famine would be expected following global war. There will be runaway inflation during this time. The buying power of money will drop dramatically. This will be a time of economic devastation and famine, during which life will be reduced to the barest necessities.

Black is an appropriate color here, for it points to the lamentation and sorrow that naturally accompany extreme deprivation. That black can represent hunger is illustrated for us in Lamentations 4:8-9: "Now their faces are blacker than soot. No one recognizes them in the streets. Their skin sticks to their bones; it is as dry and hard as wood. Those killed by the sword are better off than those who die of hunger. Starving, they waste away for lack of food from the fields."

There is one further observation we can make here. The book of Revelation tells us that those who refuse to take the mark of the beast will not be permitted to buy or sell, which means they will have much less food than everyone else (Revelation 13:16-17). As economic outcasts, believers during the tribulation will experience much hunger. These will be black days indeed.

We not only read about famine in the book of Revelation, we also read about earthquakes (just as prophesied by Jesus in the Olivet Discourse—Matthew 24:7). Revelation 6:12-14 says, "There was a great earthquake. The sun became as dark as black cloth, and the moon became as red as blood. Then the stars of the sky fell to the earth like green figs falling from a tree shaken by a strong wind. The sky was rolled up like a scroll, and all of the mountains and islands were moved from their places." There will be massive cosmic disturbances during the tribulation period.

Pervasive Death

In the Olivet Discourse, Jesus prophesied about believers being "arrested, persecuted, and killed" (Matthew 24:9). Countless people around the world will die. This is in keeping with the fourth seal judgment in the book of Revelation—also known as the fourth horseman of the apocalypse: "When the Lamb broke the fourth seal, I heard the fourth living being say, 'Come!' I looked up and saw a horse whose color was pale green. Its rider was named Death, and his companion was the Grave. These two were given authority over one-fourth of the earth, to kill with the sword and famine and disease and wild animals" (Revelation 6:7-8). The death symbolized here seems to be the natural consequence of the previous three judgments—the coming of the antichrist, war, and famine. The death toll will be catastrophic— a fourth of earth's population. No wonder the color of the fourth horse is said to be "pale green"—the color of a corpse. Woe to those who dwell on the earth during this time!

Things Will Get Worse

After Jesus prophesied false messiahs, wars and threats of wars, famines, and earthquakes, He stated, "All this is only the first of the birth pains, with more to come" (Matthew 24:8). By calling specific attention to these events as the "first of the birth pains," Jesus is indicating that there would be a marked increase in these things— in both rate and intensity—as the tribulation period unfolds.

Persecution and Martyrdom

In the Olivet Discourse, Jesus prophesied, "You will be arrested, persecuted, and killed. You will be hated all over the world because you are my followers" (Matthew 24:9). These words were spoken not about church-age believers, who will be raptured prior to the beginning of the tribulation (1 Thessalonians 1:10; 4:13-17; 5:9; Revelation 3:10), but about those who will become believers during the tribulation itself (see Matthew 25:31-46; Revelation 7:9-10).

All this is consistent with what we read in the book of Revelation—a revelation that came from Jesus Christ (Revelation 1:1-3). Revelation 13:7 tells us that "the beast [or antichrist] was allowed to wage war against God's holy people and to conquer them." Another parallel passage is Daniel 7:21, which, speaking of the antichrist, tells us that he "was waging war against God's holy people and was defeating them." Many of God's people will die during that time. The Revelation passage tells us that the antichrist will *conquer* the saints, whereas the Daniel passage tells us he will *defeat* them.

There will be many martyrs during the tribulation period. The *Believer's Bible Commentary* tells us that the antichrist "makes war with God's people and overcomes many of them. They die rather than submit to him. His rule extends over all the world—the last world empire before Christ's Reign."[1] God's people will prefer to experience death than yield to the antichrist, knowing that they will live forever with the true Christ, Jesus the divine Messiah.

Elsewhere in the book of Revelation, we read of martyrs of Christ:

> When the Lamb broke the fifth seal, I saw under the altar the souls of all who had been martyred for the word of God and for being faithful in their testimony. They shouted to the Lord and said, "O Sovereign Lord, holy and true, how long before you judge the people who belong to this world and avenge our blood for what they have done to us?" Then a white robe was given to each of them. And they were told to rest a little longer until the full number of their brothers and sisters—their fellow servants of Jesus who were to be martyred—had joined them (Revelation 6:9-11).

This passage indicates that not only will many already be martyred in the early days of the tribulation, but more would continue to be martyred. Some of these martyred "fellow servants" will comprise the "vast crowd" mentioned in Revelation 7:9-17—"the ones who died in the great tribulation," who "have washed their robes in the blood of the Lamb and made them white" (verse 14). While some of this "vast crowd" may die natural deaths, most will likely die as martyrs. Bible expositor Thomas Constable comments:

> This group appears to be the same as the one referred to earlier in 6:9-11 (cf. v. 14). These believers died either natural or violent deaths during the first half of the Tribulation. They have joined the angels in the heavenly throne-room that John saw previously (chs. 4–5; cf. v. 11). Now they hold palm branches symbolizing their victory and joy (cf. John 12:13). They are worshiping and serving God in heaven…They will no longer experience the privations and discomforts of their earthly existence (cf. Isa. 49:10, LXX; John 4:14; 6:35; 7:37). The Lamb, now seen standing before the middle of the throne, will provide for them as a good shepherd takes care of his sheep (cf. Ps. 23:1-4; Isa. 40:11; Ezek. 34:23; John 10:11, 14; Heb. 13:20; 1 Pet. 2:25; 5:2-4).[2]

The book of Revelation indicates that such martyrdom in the tribulation period will be nothing new. After all, in Revelation 2, Christ speaks to the church in Pergamum about one of His faithful martyrs: "I know that you live in the city where Satan has his throne, yet you have remained loyal to me. You refused to deny me even when Antipas, my faithful witness, was martyred among you there in Satan's city" (verse 13).

Christ urges His people to stand strong and not fear martyrdom. When He spoke words of comfort to the church in Smyrna, He exhorted them: "Don't be afraid of what you are about to suffer.

The devil will throw some of you into prison to test you. You will suffer for ten days. But if you remain faithful even when facing death, I will give you the crown of life" (Revelation 2:10).

Ultimately what this means is that even though God's people will be persecuted during the tribulation period, with some of them being put to death, death will simply serve as the gateway into life eternal—that is, life with Jesus Christ, the divine Messiah in heaven.

Global Apostasy

Jesus then addressed global apostasy in His Olivet Discourse. The word *apostasy* comes from the Greek word *apostasia*, which means "falling away." The word refers to a falling away from the truth. It depicts a determined, willful "defection from the faith," or an "abandonment of the faith." Jesus prophesied, "Many will turn away from me" (Matthew 24:10). The Amplified Bible translates it this way: "At that time many will be offended and repelled [by their association with Me] and will fall away [from the One whom they should trust]." Jesus said this turning away from Him will take place at the same time that many turn to false prophets: "Many false prophets will appear and will deceive many people" (24:11).

Jesus's words on apostasy are in keeping with those of the apostle Paul. Recall that Paul was Christ's "chosen instrument" to take His message to both Gentiles and Jews (Acts 9:15). This means that what Paul taught on end-times apostasy was actually a part of Christ's prophetic "message" to the people.

Like Jesus, Paul affirmed that there would be an increase of apostasy in the end times. For example, he warned in 1 Timothy 4:1-2, "The Holy Spirit tells us clearly that in the last times some will turn away from the true faith; they will follow deceptive spirits and teachings that come from demons. These people are hypocrites and liars, and their consciences are dead."

It is notable that a number of the cults and false religions that pepper our land today first emerged when the leaders of these groups received an alleged revelation from an "angel"—which we know to be fallen angels, or demons. A classic example is Mormonism, which was founded by Joseph Smith after he allegedly received a revelation from an angel known as Moroni. Another example is Islam, which is based on revelations that Muhammad claimed were brought to him by the angel Gabriel. In the New Age movement, God's angels are allegedly appearing to people and telling them they're free to come up with their own new religions. The examples seem endless.

Paul then warned in 2 Timothy 4:3-4, "A time is coming when people will no longer listen to sound and wholesome teaching. They will follow their own desires and will look for teachers who will tell them whatever their itching ears want to hear. They will reject the truth and chase after myths." Who can doubt that these words describe the very days in which we live? As one channel-surfs on television in the evening, one will come across examples of numerous such false teachers espousing doctrines that appeal to people's passions, such as the health-and-wealth gospel.

Paul then provided specific details on end-times apostasy in 2 Timothy 3:1-5:

> In the last days there will be very difficult times. For people will love only themselves and their money. They will be boastful and proud, scoffing at God, disobedient to their parents, and ungrateful. They will consider nothing sacred. They will be unloving and unforgiving; they will slander others and have no self-control. They will be cruel and hate what is good. They will betray their friends, be reckless, be puffed up with pride, and love pleasure rather than God. They will act religious, but they will reject the power that could make them godly. Stay away from people like that!

Paul warned that apostasy will rise to a fever pitch during the tribulation period. In 2 Thessalonians 2:3 he affirmed, "Let no one deceive you in any way. For that day will not come, unless the rebellion comes first" (ESV). Many Bible expositors believe this refers to a *rebellion against the truth.*

The deception during the tribulation period is nowhere clearer than when we compare the true Christ with the antichrist, who will rise to power during that time. The antichrist will mimic the true Christ in a number of ways:

- The true Christ performed miracles, signs, and wonders (Matthew 9:32-33; Mark 6:2); the antichrist will perform counterfeit miracles, signs, and wonders (Matthew 24:24; 2 Thessalonians 2:9).

- The true Christ will appear in the millennial temple (Ezekiel 43:6-7); the antichrist will sit in the tribulation temple (2 Thessalonians 2:4).

- The true Christ is God (John 1:1-2; 10:36); the antichrist will claim to be God (2 Thessalonians 2:4).

- The true Christ causes humans to worship God (Revelation 1:6); the antichrist will cause humans to worship Satan (Revelation 13:3-4).

- Followers of the true Christ will be sealed on their forehead (Revelation 7:4; 14:1); followers of the antichrist will be sealed on their forehead or right hand (the "mark of the beast"— Revelation 13:16-18).

- The true Christ has a worthy name (Revelation 19:16); the antichrist will have blasphemous names (Revelation 13:1).

- The true Christ will be married to a virtuous bride—the bride of Christ, or the church (Revelation 19:7-9); the antichrist will be married to a vile prostitute—a false religious system (Revelation 17:3-5).

- The true Christ will be crowned with many crowns (Revelation 19:12); the antichrist will be crowned with ten crowns (Revelation 13:1).

- The true Christ is the King of kings (Revelation 19:16); the antichrist will be called "the king" (Daniel 11:36).

- The true Christ will ride on a white horse (Revelation 19:11); the antichrist will also ride upon a white horse (Revelation 6:2).

- The true Christ resurrected from the dead (Matthew 28:6); the antichrist will experience an apparent resurrection from the dead (Revelation 13:3,14).

- The true Christ will have a 1,000-year worldwide kingdom (Revelation 20:1-6); the antichrist will have a three-and-a-half-year worldwide kingdom (Revelation 13:5-8).

- The true Christ is part of the Holy Trinity—Father, Son, and Holy Spirit (2 Corinthians 13:14); the antichrist is part of an unholy trinity—Satan, the antichrist, and the false prophet (Revelation 13).

Oh, the deception!

It is sobering to contemplate that multitudes will volitionally choose to follow the antichrist during the tribulation period. I say this because the antichrist's character is precisely opposite that of the true Christ. That so many will make this choice reveals the extent to which people will fall away from the true Christ (Matthew 24:10). The following stark contrasts between Christ and the antichrist bear this point out:

- One is called the man of sorrows (Isaiah 53:3), the other the man of sin (2 Thessalonians 2:3).

- One is called the Son of God (John 1:34), the other the son of perdition (2 Thessalonians 2:3).

- One is called the Lamb (Isaiah 53:7), the other the beast (Revelation 11:7).
- One is called the Holy One (Mark 1:24), the other the wicked one (2 Thessalonians 2:8).
- Christ came to do the Father's will (John 6:38); the antichrist will do his own will (Daniel 11:36).
- Christ was energized by the Holy Spirit (Luke 4:14); the antichrist will be energized by Satan, the unholy spirit (Revelation 13:4).
- Christ submitted Himself to God (John 5:30); the antichrist will defy God (2 Thessalonians 2:4).
- Christ humbled Himself (Philippians 2:8); the antichrist will exalt himself (Daniel 11:37).
- Christ honored the God of His fathers (Luke 4:16); the antichrist will refuse to honor God (Daniel 11:37).
- Christ cleansed the temple (John 2:14,16); the antichrist will defile the temple (Matthew 24:15).
- Christ was rejected of men (Isaiah 53:7); the antichrist will—by force—be accepted by men (Revelation 13:4).
- Christ was slain for the people (John 11:51); the antichrist will slay the people (Isaiah 14:20).
- Christ was received up into heaven (Luke 24:51); the antichrist will go down into the lake of fire (Revelation 19:20).

Clearly, then, the multitudes who will turn away from Christ during the tribulation period will, at the same time, turn toward the ultimate false Christ—*the antichrist*. The apostasy will be staggering.

Now, please allow me to share an observation with you. The prophetic Scriptures reveal that the antichrist will be energized and empowered by Satan (2 Thessalonians 2:9). We learn from the Bible that Satan is the "father of lies" (John 8:44). Satan is a master deceiver, and is the greatest among all liars. His lies are typically religious in nature, distorting the biblical picture of God, Jesus, and the true gospel. Because Satan is the father of lies, it makes sense that the one whom he energizes—the antichrist—will also be characterized by lies and deception.

Not only will the antichrist be full of deception, but Satan—the god of this world—will have "blinded the minds of those who don't believe. They are unable to see the glorious light of the Good News. They don't understand this message about the glory of Christ, who is the exact likeness of God" (2 Corinthians 4:4).

Tragically, because unbelievers will have turned their backs on God, God will hand them over to a powerful delusion. While God desires all to be saved (1 Timothy 2:4-6), many refuse God's truth and offer of salvation. When that happens, God eventually allows them to experience the full brunt of the consequences of falsehood (see Romans 1:18-25). The context of the book of Revelation indicates that people will experience the full consequences of falsehood during the second half of the tribulation, also known as the "great tribulation."

The Good News Preached to All Nations

In the Olivet Discourse, Jesus prophesied that "the Good News about the Kingdom will be preached throughout the whole world, so that all nations will hear it" (Matthew 24:14). Jesus's prophetic revelations in the book of Revelation tell us about the preachers of this gospel—144,000 Jews, with 12,000 from each of the twelve tribes of Israel (Revelation 7; 14).

The backdrop to a proper understanding of the 144,000 is that God had originally chosen the Jews to be His witnesses, their appointed task being to share the good news of God with all other people around the world (see Isaiah 42:6; 43:10). The Jews were to be God's representatives to the Gentile peoples. Biblical history reveals that the Jews failed at this task, especially since they did not even recognize Jesus as the divine Messiah, but nevertheless this was their calling. During the future tribulation, these 144,000 Jews—who will become believers sometime following the rapture—will finally fulfill this mandate from God and serve as His witnesses all around the world. They will globally share the good news about the kingdom. Their work will yield a mighty harvest of souls (see Revelation 7:9-14).

We are told these witnesses will be protectively "sealed" by God. They will be divinely protected as they preach the gospel of the kingdom during the tribulation (Revelation 14:1,3-4; see also 7:4).

Just as John the Baptist and Jesus often preached a message that communicated the kingdom of God is near, so will God's 144,000 witnesses do the same during the tribulation period. Jesus Christ will be clearly presented as the divine Messiah, the King who will rule in the coming millennial kingdom. Bible expositors William MacDonald and Arthur L. Farstad note, "The gospel of the kingdom is the good news that Christ is coming to set up His kingdom on earth, and that those who receive Him by faith during the Tribulation will enjoy the blessings of His Millennial Reign."[3]

Those who turn to the King during the tribulation period will be granted entrance into Christ's 1,000-year millennial kingdom, while those who reject Him will be forbidden entrance. Indeed, at the judgment that takes place following Christ's second coming, Christ will divide all people "as a shepherd separates the sheep from the goats" (Matthew 25:32). The sheep (believers) will be invited into Christ's millennial kingdom, whereas the goats (unbelievers) will be sent into punishment (see Matthew 25:31-46).

The book of Revelation reveals that many will respond to this gospel of the kingdom. In the end, there will be "a vast crowd, too great to count, from every nation and tribe and people and language, standing in front of the throne and before the Lamb. They were clothed in white robes and held palm branches in their hands. And they were shouting with a great roar, 'Salvation comes from our God who sits on the throne and from the Lamb!'" (Revelation 7:9-10).

Despite this good news, there is still much to address about the horror yet to come during the tribulation period. We will continue our discussion of this in the next chapter.

3

The Tribulation Period, Part 2

We began our overview of Jesus's teachings on the tribulation period in the previous chapter. We addressed the notable parallels between Jesus's prophetic teachings in the Olivet Discourse and those found in the book of Revelation: false Christs, wars and threats of wars, famines and earthquakes, pervasive death, persecution and martyrdom, global apostasy, and the preaching of the good news to all the nations of the world. We now continue our discussion, first addressing a detestable act of the antichrist that is known as "the abomination of desolation."

The Abomination of Desolation

Jesus prophesied the desecration of the Jewish temple during the tribulation period: "The day is coming when you will see what Daniel the prophet spoke about—the sacrilegious object that causes desecration standing in the Holy Place" (Matthew 24:15). Jesus was referring to Daniel 11:31, where the prophet Daniel said that the antichrist's army "will take over the Temple fortress, pollute the sanctuary, put a stop to the daily sacrifices, and set up the sacrilegious object that causes desecration."

Daniel 9:27 adds further clarity by revealing that the act of desecration takes place at the midpoint of the future tribulation period. At this time, the antichrist—the "man of lawlessness" (2 Thessalonians 2:4)—will set up an image of himself inside the Jewish temple (see Daniel 9:27; Matthew 24:15). This will be utterly detestable to the Jews. The word *abomination* comes from a root term that means "to make foul" or "to stink." Thus it refers to something that makes one feel nauseous, and by implication, something morally abhorrent and detestable.

The antichrist's sacrilegious act will amount to enthroning himself in the place of deity, displaying himself as God (compare with Isaiah 14:13-14 and Ezekiel 28:2-9). This blasphemous act will utterly desecrate the temple, making it abominable, and therefore desolate. The antichrist—the world dictator—will then demand that the world worship and pay idolatrous homage to him. Any who refuse will be persecuted and even martyred. The false prophet, who will be the antichrist's first lieutenant, will see to this.

The fact that the antichrist will "put a stop to the daily sacrifices" in the Jewish temple (Daniel 11:31) is yet another indication of his self-exaltation. He will not allow competing systems of worship to exist. From this point onward, no one is to be worshipped but him alone.

The fact that the antichrist will claim to be God is in line with the fact that he will be energized by Satan (2 Thessalonians 2:9), who himself had earlier sought godhood (Isaiah 14:13-14; Ezekiel 28:2-9). The antichrist will take on the character of the one who will energize him. As Bible expositor Renald Showers put it, by the middle of the seventieth week, the antichrist "will turn against every form of established worship to clear the way for the worship of himself. He will magnify himself to the level of deity."[1]

An abomination on a much lesser scale took place back in 168 BC. At that time, Antiochus Epiphanies—then ruler of the

Seleucid Empire, and a cruel persecutor of the Jews—erected an altar to Zeus in the temple at Jerusalem and sacrificed a pig (an unclean animal) upon it. Antiochus may be considered a prototype of the future antichrist.

Now, please allow me to clarify that Jesus was not saying that the abomination of desolation would take place in the Jewish temple *of His day*. After all, Jesus positively affirmed that the great temple built by Herod (the Jewish temple of Jesus's day) would be utterly destroyed: "Do you see all these buildings? I tell you the truth, they will be completely demolished. Not one stone will be left on top of another!" This prophecy was literally fulfilled in AD 70 when Titus and his Roman warriors overran Jerusalem and the Jewish temple.

The only conclusion that can be reached is that though the temple of Jesus's day would be destroyed, the abomination of desolation would occur in a yet-future temple (Matthew 24:15). This latter temple would be built by the middle of the tribulation period (see also Daniel 9:27; 12:11).

There is one further observation to make here. Recall that during His three-year ministry, Jesus cleansed the temple (Mark 11:15-19). By contrast, the antichrist will defile the temple when he sits "in the temple of God, claiming that he himself is God" (2 Thessalonians 2:4). Truly the antichrist will be a detestable antithesis of the true Christ.

The Jews Escape from Jerusalem

Once the Jews in Jerusalem witness the "sacrilegious object that causes desecration standing in the Holy Place" (Matthew 24:15), Jesus prophetically urges them,

> Those in Judea must flee to the hills. A person out on the deck of a roof must not go down into the house to pack. A person out in the field must not return even to get a coat.

How terrible it will be for pregnant women and for nurs-
ing mothers in those days. And pray that your flight will
not be in winter or on the Sabbath. For there will be greater
anguish than at any time since the world began. And it will
never be so great again (Matthew 24:16-22).

Let's unpack this passage a bit. When these horrific circumstances unfold in Jerusalem, Jesus urges that the Jews living there
should have no concern whatsoever for personal belongings, but
rather they should make haste to get out of town with utmost speed.
They are to literally run for their lives. Time spent in gathering personal belongings might mean the difference between life and death.
Jesus indicates that the distress will escalate dramatically and rapidly. Jeremiah 30:7 describes this period as "a time of trouble for my
people Israel."

It appears that Revelation 12:5-6 alludes to this time of trouble for Israel. This verse metaphorically refers to Israel as a "woman"
who had given birth "to a son" (Jesus Christ). We are told that "the
woman fled into the wilderness, where God had prepared a place
to care for her for 1,260 days." These Jews apparently will flee to
the deserts and mountains, perhaps in the area of Bozrah or Petra,
about 80 miles south of Jerusalem. Others suggest Moab, Ammon,
and Edom to the east.

The Lord will take care of this remnant of Jews in the wilderness
for 1,260 days, which is precisely three-and-a-half years—the last
half of the tribulation period.

Revelation 12:13-16 then tells us:

When the dragon realized that he had been thrown down
to the earth, he pursued the woman who had given birth to
the male child. But she was given two wings like those of a
great eagle so she could fly to the place prepared for her in
the wilderness. There she would be cared for and protected
from the dragon for a time, times, and half a time.

> Then the dragon tried to drown the woman with a flood of
> water that flowed from his mouth. But the earth helped her
> by opening its mouth and swallowing the river that gushed
> out from the mouth of the dragon.

Once Satan is ousted from heaven and is thrown down to the earth at the midpoint of the tribulation period, he will seek to violently persecute the Jews, from whose lineage the Messiah was born. This persecution will no doubt be carried out through the instrument of the antichrist (Daniel 9:27; Matthew 24:15; 2 Thessalonians 2:4). The antichrist will be Satan's puppet.

Interestingly, Scripture reveals that Jesus will not return until the Jewish people are endangered at Armageddon and the Jewish leaders cry out for deliverance from the divine Messiah (see Zechariah 12:10). Satan, in his perverted thinking, may reason that if he can destroy the Jews, he can thereby prevent their calling out to the divine Messiah, and hence prevent the second coming of Christ, thus saving himself from defeat.

Our passage tells us that the woman "was given two wings like those of a great eagle so she could fly to the place prepared for her in the wilderness" (Revelation 12:14). Wings often represent protection and deliverance in the Bible (see Psalm 91:4; Isaiah 40:31). For example, after God delivered the Jews from Egyptian bondage, He affirmed, "You have seen what I did to the Egyptians. You know how I carried you on eagles' wings and brought you to myself" (Exodus 19:4). Therefore, the "two wings" in Revelation 12:14 point to God's supernatural delivering power.

While God will preserve a remnant of Jews through this time of persecution, this should not be taken to mean that all the Jews will survive. According to Zechariah the prophet, "Two-thirds of the people in the land will be cut off and die...But one-third will be left in the land" (Zechariah 13:8). Many will die, but a remnant will survive the onslaught.

This remnant will be "protected from the dragon for a time, times, and half a time" (that is, one year, plus two years, plus half a year) (Revelation 12:14). In other words, God will preserve the Jews throughout the last three-and-a-half years of the tribulation period (see Daniel 7:25; 12:7).

We are then told that "the dragon tried to drown the woman with a flood of water that flowed from his mouth" (Revelation 12:15). Some Bible expositors take this to mean that Satan will cause a literal flood of water in an attempt to dislodge and destroy the Jews. Others take the flood metaphorically, suggesting that a satanically driven army will rapidly advance against the Jews like a flood. It may also refer more broadly to an outpouring of hatred and anti-Semitism.

Our text then goes on to tell us that "the earth helped her by opening its mouth and swallowing the river that gushed out from the mouth of the dragon" (Revelation 12:16). Whichever of the above interpretations is correct, the earth, under God's providence, will come to the aid of the Jews. If the flood is literal water, perhaps God will cause the earth to open up and swallow the water. If the flood is a rapidly advancing army (or militant anti-Semitics), perhaps these people will be destroyed by an earthquake that causes the ground to open up (see Matthew 24:7; Revelation 6:12; 8:5; 11:13,19; 16:18).

We must never forget God's promise to the Jews in Isaiah 54:17: "No weapon turned against you will succeed." Not even water, literal or metaphorical. Moreover, "he who watches over Israel never slumbers or sleeps. The LORD himself watches over you! The LORD stands beside you as your protective shade" (Psalm 121:4-5).

A Sovereign Shortening of the Time of Calamity

Jesus spoke these prophetic words about the last three-and-a-half years of the tribulation period: "There will be greater anguish than at any time since the world began. And it will never be so great again"

(Matthew 24:21). Jesus then said, "In fact, unless that time of calamity is shortened, not a single person will survive. But it will be shortened for the sake of God's chosen ones" (verse 22). Was Jesus saying He would make the second half of the tribulation period *shorter* than three-and-a-half years, or was He saying that the three-and-a-half years was, in itself, the shortened time?

To answer this question, we turn to the parallel verse in Mark 13:20: "Unless the Lord shortens that time of calamity, not a single person will survive. But for the sake of his chosen ones he has shortened those days." Greek scholars note that the verbs in this verse express action that was taken by God in the past. This means that God, in eternity past, sovereignly decreed a limitation on the length of the great tribulation.

We conclude that Jesus was teaching that God in the past had *already shortened* the great tribulation. He did so in the sense that in the past, He sovereignly decreed to cut it off at a specific time rather than let it continue indefinitely. In His omniscience, God knew that if the great tribulation were to continue indefinitely, all humanity would perish. To prevent that from happening, God, in eternity past, "sovereignly fixed a specific time for the Great Tribulation to end—when it had run its course for three and one-half years or 42 months or 1,260 days. That fixed time cannot be changed."[2]

False Messiahs, False Prophets, and Signs and Wonders

Jesus's next prophecy in the Olivet Discourse addressed the rise of false Christs, false prophets, and their counterfeit signs and wonders: "Then if anyone tells you, 'Look, here is the Messiah,' or 'There he is,' don't believe it. For false messiahs and false prophets will rise up and perform great signs and wonders so as to deceive, if possible, even God's chosen ones. See, I have warned you about this ahead of time. So if someone tells you, 'Look, the Messiah is out in the desert,' don't bother to go and look. Or, 'Look, he is hiding here,' don't believe it!" (Matthew 24:23-26). While there's no doubt that a number of false Christs and false prophets will emerge in the end times, the book of Revelation zeros in on the one definitive false Christ—*the antichrist*—along with his first lieutenant, the false prophet (see Revelation 13).

This reminds us that in the theology of John—the same John who recorded Christ's revelations in the book of Revelation—we are informed about "antichrists," "the antichrist," and the "spirit of antichrist." Let's examine each of these in more detail.

The Spirit of Antichrist. The "spirit of antichrist" was at work even back in John's day, promoting heretical and cultic doctrine. Based on John's writings, we can surmise that the spirit of antichrist promotes deception (2 John 7), denies that Christ came in the flesh (1 John 4:2-3), denies the Father and the Son (1 John 2:22), was already in the world (1 John 4:3), was prevalent in apostolic times (1 John 2:18), and is closely related to false prophets (1 John 4:1).

Many theologians believe that the "spirit of antichrist" refers to demonic spirits who promulgate anti-Christian teachings (1 John 4:3). In keeping with this, 1 Timothy 4:1 warns, "The Holy Spirit tells us clearly that in the last times some will turn away from the true faith; they will follow deceptive spirits and teachings that come from demons."

In their book *Global Warning*, Tim LaHaye and Ed Hindson note that the spirit of antichrist has been active in every century of church history:

> The New Testament authors assure us that the "spirit of antichrist" was active in their day over 20 centuries ago. It has remained active throughout the whole of church history, expressing itself in persecutions, heresies, spiritual deceptions, false prophets, and false religions. Satan has battled the church at every turn throughout its long history,

waiting for the right moment to indwell the right person—the Antichrist—as his final masterpiece.[3]

Many Antichrists. In 1 John 2:18, the apostle John warned, "Dear children, the last hour is here. You have heard that the Antichrist is coming, and already many such antichrists have appeared. From this we know that the last hour has come." What does John mean by this statement?

Contextually, the entire time span between the first and second comings of Christ constitute "the last hour" (see 1 Timothy 4:1; James 5:3; 1 Peter 4:7; 2 Peter 3:3; Jude 18). During this time span, various manifestations of "antichrist" have emerged.

For example, as one who has written many books on the kingdom of the cults, I can tell you with some authority that without exception, the various cults all present heretical views of Jesus Christ—His person, His words, His works, and His resurrection. All such false religious groups throughout church history are the work of "antichrists." Such individuals may be considered wolves in sheep's clothing, proliferating damaging lies (see Ephesians 5:11).

The Antichrist. As opposed to the many antichrists of church history, Scripture reveals that there is a single individual known as "the antichrist" who is yet to come, and will emerge into power during the future tribulation period (see Daniel 8:9-11; 11:31-38; 12:11; Matthew 24:15; 2 Thessalonians 2:1-12; Revelation 13:1-5). This individual will be the embodiment of all that is anti-God and anti-Christian. He will be the supreme antichrist of human history.

The term *anti* in *antichrist* means "instead of," "against," and "opposed to." More than any other, the antichrist will position himself as "instead of" Christ, "against" Christ, and "opposed to" Christ. He will set himself up against Christ and the people of God in the last days before the second coming.

This Satan-inspired individual will rise to prominence in the tribulation period by making a peace treaty with Israel (Daniel 9:27). But then he will double-cross and seek to destroy the Jews, as well as persecute believers, seek to dominate the world, and set up his own kingdom (Revelation 13). He will speak arrogant and boastful words in glorifying himself (2 Thessalonians 2:4). His assistant, the false prophet, will seek to make the world worship him (Revelation 13:11-12). People around the world will be forced to receive his mark, without which they cannot buy or sell, thereby enabling the antichrist to control the global economy (Revelation 13:16-17). However, to receive this mark ensures one of being the recipient of God's wrath. The antichrist will eventually rule the whole world (Revelation 13:7), with his headquarters in Rome (Revelation 17:8-9). This beast will be defeated and destroyed by Jesus at His second coming (Revelation 19:11-16).

The Escalation of Cosmic Disturbances

Jesus continued His Olivet Discourse by prophesying about various cosmic disturbances that will occur during the end times: "Immediately after the anguish of those days, the sun will be darkened, the moon will give no light, the stars will fall from the sky, and the powers in the heavens will be shaken" (Matthew 24:29). We witness similar prophecies in association with the sixth seal judgment in the book of Revelation:

> I watched as the Lamb broke the sixth seal, and there was a great earthquake. The sun became as dark as black cloth, and the moon became as red as blood. Then the stars of the sky fell to the earth like green figs falling from a tree shaken by a strong wind. The sky was rolled up like a scroll, and all of the mountains and islands were moved from their places (Revelation 6:12-14).

The earthquake associated with the sixth seal will be so severe that all the earth's faults will begin to fracture simultaneously with devastating worldwide effects. With the earth being shaken to its core, many volcanic eruptions will likely spew huge amounts of ash and debris into the atmosphere. This may be what causes the sun to darken and the moon to appear red (see Joel 2:31).

There are other earthquakes mentioned in the book of Revelation. Revelation 11:13 speaks of a "terrible earthquake" that will kill 7,000 people. Revelation 16:18 likewise tells us, "A great earthquake struck—the worst since people were placed on the earth." Earthquakes in the book of Revelation are connected with judgment; each of the three series of judgments—the seal judgments, the trumpet judgments, and the bowl judgments—ends with an earthquake.

Related to this discussion of earthquakes, Scripture reveals that in the end times, a northern military coalition involving Russia, Iran, Turkey, Sudan, Libya, and other Muslim nations will invade Israel (see Ezekiel 38), and God Himself will destroy these invaders. One of the means by which God will do this is through a great earthquake (verses 19-20). The devastating earthquake described by Ezekiel—in which "mountains will be thrown down; cliffs will crumble; walls will fall to the earth"—will cause many troops to die, and transportation will be severely disrupted. Apparently the armies of the multinational forces will be thrown into utter chaos. So intense will this earthquake be that all the creatures on the earth will feel its effect (verse 20).

As noted previously, the sixth seal judgment entails other cosmic disturbances besides earthquakes. We read that "the stars of the sky fell to the earth like green figs falling from a tree shaken by a strong wind" (Revelation 6:13). This apparently refers to asteroids or meteor showers.

Then "the sky was rolled up like a scroll" (Revelation 6:14). The earth's atmosphere will be catastrophically affected by all these judgments (compare with Isaiah 34:4). Perhaps the terminology indicates simply that with all the dust and debris, people will not be able to see the sky anymore, thus causing great fear on the earth.

It is understandable that "mountains and islands" will be moved from their places (Revelation 6:14). With all the earth's faults fracturing simultaneously, the earth's plates will shift, thereby causing the actual landscape of the earth to change.

Woe unto people living during these days!

What About the Preterist Interpretation of Jesus's Prophetic Words?

The word *preterism* derives from the Latin *preter*, meaning "past." Those who hold to the preterist view of the biblical prophecies in the book of Revelation (especially chapters 6–18) and Matthew 24–25 (Christ's Olivet Discourse) say these prophecies have already been fulfilled in the past. This approach to interpreting prophecy was held by the early writer Eusebius (AD 263–339) in his *Ecclesiastical History*. Later writers who incorporated this approach include Hugo Grotius of Holland (ca. 1644) and, in modern times, David Chilton.

There are two forms of preterism. Moderate preterism is represented by modern writers such as R.C. Sproul, Hank Hanegraaff, and Gary DeMar. While they believe the literal resurrection and second coming are yet future, the other prophecies in Revelation and Matthew 24–25 have allegedly already been fulfilled when Titus and his Roman warriors overran Jerusalem and destroyed the Jewish temple in AD 70. Hence, most of the book of Revelation does not deal with the future.

Extreme or full preterism goes so far as to say that *all* New Testament predictions were fulfilled in the past, including those of the resurrection and second coming. This latter view is heretical, denying two of the fundamentals of the faith: the physical resurrection and a literal second coming.

Preterists often point to Matthew 24:34, where Jesus asserted, "I tell you the truth, this generation will not pass from the scene until all these things take place." They claim this verse proves the prophecies would be fulfilled in the first century.

Contrary to this idea, evangelical Christians have generally held to one of two interpretations of Matthew 24:34. One is that Christ was simply saying that those people who witness the signs stated earlier in Matthew 24—the abomination of desolation (verse 15), the great tribulation such as has never been seen before (verse 21), and the sign of the Son of Man in heaven (verse 30)—will see the coming of Jesus Christ within that very generation. Since it was common knowledge among the Jews that the future tribulation period would last only seven years (Daniel 9:24-27), it is obvious that those living at the beginning of this time would likely live to see the second coming seven years later (except for those who lose their lives during this tumultuous time).

Other evangelicals hold that Christ's use of "generation" is to be understood in the sense of "race," "kindred," or "family." If this is what is meant, then Jesus was promising that the nation of Israel would be preserved—despite terrible persecution during the tribulation—until the consummation of God's program for Israel at the second coming. Many divine promises have been made to Israel—including land promises (Genesis 12; 14–15; 17) and the assurance of a future Davidic kingdom (2 Samuel 7). Jesus could thus be referring to God's preservation of Israel in order to fulfill the divine promises made to them (see Romans 11:11-26). Either way, Matthew 24:34 does not support preterism.

Preterists also argue from Matthew 16:28 that Jesus said some of His followers "standing here right now" would not taste death until they saw Him return, "coming in his Kingdom." These preterists argue that prophecies of the second coming must have been fulfilled during their generation—apparently in AD 70 when Rome overran Jerusalem.

Contrary to this view, many evangelicals believe that when Jesus said this, He had in mind the transfiguration, which happened one week later (Matthew 17:1-13). According to this view, the transfiguration served as a preview of the kingdom in which the divine Messiah would appear in glory. Moreover, against the idea that this verse refers to AD 70 is the pivotal fact that some of the disciples "standing" there were no longer alive by AD 70 (all but John had been martyred by then). Still further, no astronomical events occurred in AD 70, such as the stars falling from heaven and the heavens being shaken (Matthew 24:29). And Jesus did not return "on the clouds of heaven with power and great glory" (Matthew 24:30). The preterist understanding of Matthew 16:28 does not sync with many of the prophetic scriptures.

Preterists try to rebut that some Bible verses indicate that Jesus will come "soon" or "quickly." For example, in Revelation 22:12 Jesus said, "Look, I am coming soon, bringing my reward with me to repay all people according to their deeds." Jesus also said, "Yes, I am coming soon!" (verse 20). In keeping with this, Revelation 1:1 affirms, "This is a revelation from Jesus Christ, which God gave him to show his servants the events that must soon take place." In Revelation 22:6 we read, "The Lord God, who inspires his prophets, has sent his angel to tell his servants what will happen soon." How are we to take such verses?

A consultation of the original Greek text in the book of Revelation clears everything up. The reality is that the Greek word translated "soon" in these verses carries the idea of "swiftly," "speedily," or "at a rapid rate." Hence, the term could simply indicate that when the predicted events first start to occur, they will then progress swiftly, in rapid succession.

A favorite argument among preterists is that the book of Revelation was written prior to AD 70, and that the book must have been fulfilled in AD 70 when Rome overran Jerusalem. Futurists point out, however, that some of the earliest church fathers confirmed a late date of Revelation, including Irenaeus, who claimed the book was written at the close of the reign of Domitian (which took place from AD 81–96). Victorinus confirmed this date in the third century, as did Eusebius (AD 263–340). Hence, since the book was written *after* AD 70, it could hardly have been referring to events that would be fulfilled *in* AD 70. All things considered, preterist arguments are unconvincing.

In the next chapter, we will continue our study of the tribulation period as we turn our attention to the famous parable of the fig tree.

4

Be Alert: The Parable of the Fig Tree

Fig trees were as common to people in Bible times as palm trees are to modern Californians and Hawaiians. Palestine was brimming with fig trees. They were found in many family yards, and were a great source of delicious fruit. They also provided much-needed shade during the hot summer months.

Jesus was a master at speaking in terms His listeners would understand. That's why He made use of word pictures—often using something in the natural world to illustrate some particular truth. On several occasions, He used the fig tree to illustrate truths—as he did with the parable of the fig tree (in which He urged tribulation saints to be ready for the Lord's coming), and earlier when He caused a fig tree to wither (at which time He taught that God will judge those who give an outer appearance of fruitfulness but in fact are not fruitful at all—like the Pharisees).

It's intriguing that the fig tree had been used throughout biblical history to illustrate or represent various things. John MacArthur offers this interesting insight:

> Jews were used to the fig tree's functioning as an illustration. Jotham used it in his story shouted to the inhabitants of

Shechem from the top of Mount Gerizim (Judg. 9:10-11); Jeremiah saw two baskets of figs in his vision after Nebuchadnezzar took captives from Judah to Babylon (Jer. 24:1-10); Hosea used it as a figure in his prophecy about Israel (Hos. 9:10); and Joel used a splintered fig tree to illustrate the devastation of Judah by a plague of locusts (Joel 1:4-7)...Few figures would have been better known to the disciples than [Matthew 24–28] that of the fig tree, which Jesus Himself had used on numerous other occasions as a teaching aid (see Matt. 7:16; 21:19; Luke 13:6-9).[1]

In the Olivet Discourse, Jesus appealed to the fig tree to illustrate watchfulness and readiness for the Lord's second coming:

Now learn a lesson from the fig tree. When its branches bud and its leaves begin to sprout, you know that summer is near. In the same way, when you see all these things, you can know his return is very near, right at the door. I tell you the truth, this generation will not pass from the scene until all these things take place. Heaven and earth will disappear, but my words will never disappear (Matthew 24:32-35).

Lessons Impart Wisdom

Notice how Jesus begins: "Now *learn a lesson* from the fig tree" (Matthew 24:32). In the Hebrew mindset, learning lessons was necessary for the acquiring of practical wisdom. For example, Solomon—the wisest man who ever lived (1 Kings 4:30)—urged, "Take a lesson from the ants, you lazybones. Learn from their ways and become wise!" (Proverbs 6:6). He likewise taught, "If you punish a mocker, the simpleminded will learn a lesson; if you correct the wise, they will be all the wiser" (Proverbs 19:25). The entire book of Proverbs focuses on the learning of wisdom so that one can become more skilled in the art of living.

God certainly desires wisdom among His people. We are

reminded of how He constantly desired the wayward Israelites to learn the lesson of obedience to Him, for such obedience is wise indeed. God commanded the prophet Jeremiah, "This is what the LORD of Heaven's Armies, the God of Israel, says: Go and say to the people in Judah and Jerusalem, 'Come and learn a lesson about how to obey me'" (Jeremiah 35:13).

Jesus likewise taught lessons that lead to wisdom, often through parables. In one such parable, Jesus urged, "Learn a lesson from this unjust judge" (Luke 18:6). This parable imparts wisdom related to God's justice and righteousness.

Now, here's the point I'm building up to: When Jesus said, "Learn a lesson from the fig tree" (Matthew 24:32), He wanted to communicate practical wisdom to those who become believers during the future tribulation period. Why is it important that these believers attain such wisdom? The answer is rooted in what Jesus had just shared in verses 1-31—that is, the tribulation period is going to be a horrible time to be alive on planet Earth.

During the tribulation period there will be false messiahs, wars and threats of wars, nations at war with other nations, famines, earthquakes, persecution, and martyrdom. There will also be false prophets, massive deception, rampant sin, the desecration of the Jewish temple, great anguish, a darkened sun, a moon that gives no light, stars falling from the sky, and much more. Knowing how difficult it will be to live on the earth during this time, Jesus exhorts His tribulation followers to "learn a lesson" designed to impart wisdom.

Here's something important: The Greek word translated "learn" (*manthano*) carries the idea of genuinely understanding something, accepting it as true, and then applying it to one's life. In some contexts, the word refers to the acquiring of a lifelong habit that has bearing on how one lives. Seen in this light, the learning Jesus spoke of in His parable points not merely to head knowledge, but to life-changing knowledge. The parable of the fig tree is intended to communicate a life-transforming truth to Christ's followers who live during the tribulation period.

The life-changing truth is essentially this: The one thing that can give a tribulation saint a correct understanding and perspective on the horrible circumstances that characterize the tribulation period is Jesus's prophetic words in the Olivet Discourse. By understanding Jesus's "signs of the times," believers can anchor themselves on the reality that the second coming is drawing near, and therefore they ought to remain steadfast in faithfulness.

When the Branch Buds...

In teaching His lesson from the fig tree, Jesus began by affirming, "When its branches bud and its leaves begin to sprout, you know that summer is near" (Matthew 24:32). Unlike most trees in Palestine, fig trees lose their leaves in the winter. When leaves grow on the fig trees in the spring, it is a sure sign that summer is near. Even young Jewish children in Bible times knew that a budding fig tree was a sure indication that summer was near. Likewise, when one witnesses the signs mentioned previously in the Olivet Discourse, one can perceive that Christ's coming is drawing near.

Of course, an awareness of the signs of the times requires that a person (1) knows what the signs are, as listed in the Olivet Discourse; and (2) is watching for those signs to emerge. Jesus wants His followers to be accurate observers of the times so that when biblical prophecies come to pass, they'll recognize it (see also Luke 21:25-28).

I am reminded of Jesus's comments to the Pharisees and Sadducees who missed the signs of the times as related to His first coming. Consider His words in Matthew 16:1-3:

> The Pharisees and Sadducees came up, and testing Jesus, they asked Him to show them a sign from heaven. But He replied to them, "When it is evening, you say, 'It will be fair weather, for the sky is red.' And in the morning, 'There will

be a storm today, for the sky is red and threatening.' Do you know how to discern the appearance of the sky, but cannot discern the signs of the times?"

What a rebuke! The religious elite of the time—the Pharisees and the Sadducees—were supposed to know the prophetic teachings of Scripture, and yet they were completely blind to properly discerning the times. These Jewish leaders had witnessed firsthand the "signs of the times" relating to Christ's first coming, and they had missed their significance. They had failed to recognize that the Messiah was now in their midst. The prophesied messianic miracles that Jesus wrought—giving sight to the blind, enabling the deaf to hear, and enabling the lame to walk—were just as clear an indication that He was the Messiah as dark clouds in the sky are a sign of impending rain. These miracles had been clearly prophesied of the Messiah in the Old Testament (Isaiah 35:5-6), and the Pharisees and Sadducees—experts in the Old Testament—should have seen Jesus as being the fulfillment of these messianic verses. In their blindness and hardness of heart, however, they could not discern the signs of the times.

The lesson we learn is that God's people who live during the future seven-year tribulation period ought to resolve not to follow the horrible example set by the Pharisees and Sadducees. They should not be blind to the signs of the times. As the parable of the fig tree instructs, they should watch for *specific* signs of the times to unfold—that is, the signs enumerated in Jesus's Olivet Discourse—and to consider these as pointers to the soon coming of the Lord.

An Alternate Interpretation

Some Christians take the parable differently. In their thinking, the parable of the fig tree relates to the rebirth and revival of Israel in the holy land. The fig tree is taken as "a type" of Israel, and the budding of the fig tree represents Israel's rebirth as a nation. (A *type* may be defined as a figure or representation of something, and is often used in a prophetic way.) Popular Bible teacher Warren Wiersbe exemplifies this viewpoint: "The fig tree is a symbol of Israel (Luke 13:6-10; Joel 1:6-7; Hosea 9:10). When we see Israel 'coming back to life,' then we know His return is approaching. This may be happening in our day."[2] Bible expositor Harold L. Willmington makes the same point.[3]

Other Bible expositors find this viewpoint problematic. Lewis Sperry Chafer, the first president of Dallas Theological Seminary, says,

> It is doubtless true that the fig tree represents in other Scriptures the nation Israel (cf. Matt. 21:18-20), but there is no occasion for this meaning to be sought in the present use of that symbol [in the Olivet Discourse]. When the things of which Christ had just spoken, including even the beginnings of travail, begin to come to pass, it may be accepted as certain that He is nigh, even at the doors.[4]

John F. Walvoord, Dallas Seminary's second president, agrees with Chafer's assessment:

> Because the fig tree by its nature brings forth leaves late in spring, seeing leaves on a fig tree is evidence that summer is very near. This illustration is carried over to the second coming of Christ. When the events described in the preceding verses occur, it will be a clear indication of the second coming of Christ being near. The sign in the passage is not the revival of Israel, which is not the subject of Matthew 24, but rather the details of the great tribulation.[5]

John MacArthur says it a bit more forcefully:

> Unfortunately, this parable, like many others, has often been made confusing and misleading by those who view it as a complicated allegory rather than a simple analogy.

Some interpreters, for instance, contend that the fig tree represents Israel. A popular version of that view is that the budding of the fig tree refers to Israel's becoming a political state in 1948. Because Jesus does not identify the fig tree as Israel, that meaning would have been totally obscured to the disciples and to every other believer who lived before the twentieth century.[6]

Still other scholars take a more mediating approach, suggesting that perhaps both views may have some element of truth. In other words, perhaps the parable is intended to communicate that when one witnesses the specific prophetic signs of the tribulation period that are listed in the Olivet Discourse, *and* Israel is back in the land, then all this compositely points to the soon coming of the Lord. Bible expositor Thomas Constable seems to be in this camp:

> A popular interpretation of this parable equates modern Israel's presence in the Promised Land with the budding of the fig tree. This view may be placing too much emphasis on the identification of the fig tree with the modern State of Israel (cf. Jer. 24:1-8; 29:17). On the other hand, this could be at least part of what Jesus intended.[7]

My personal assessment is that the parable of the fig tree has nothing to do with Israel's rebirth in the land, for that issue is nowhere present in the context of Matthew 24. Rather, the passage lists the specific prophetic signs that serve as pointers indicating that the second coming of Christ is drawing near. Israel's national rebirth is prophesied elsewhere in Scripture (see Ezekiel 37).

One Bible teacher I've always admired and appreciated as a *contextual* interpreter of Scripture is J. Dwight Pentecost (what a great name!). He observed,

> During the winter months the trees were bare. People who had endured the long, cold, damp winter were looking

forward to the coming of summer. As they walked along a path, they would see the first tender green shoot on a fig tree, or on any tree. This green growth was a sign to them that what they were longing for, and what they knew eventually would come, was not far off. A process had begun that would eventuate in summer. This universal principle was applied by Christ when He said, "Even so, when you see all these things, you know that it [or better, He] is near, right at the door" (Matt. 24:33). By "these things" Christ was referring to all the signs given in verses 4-26.[8]

Does the Parable of the Fig Tree Point to the Rapture?

From time to time, I come across Bible interpreters who believe the parable of the fig tree indicates the rapture is near. They suggest that we currently seem to be experiencing a fulfillment—or at least a partial fulfillment—of some of the signs of the times listed in Matthew 24, such as wars, deceptions, earthquakes, and the like. Hence, just as budding leaves on a fig tree show that summer is near, so these signs of the times must indicate the rapture is near.

The oversight of such interpreters is that the *entire* Olivet Discourse contextually deals with the tribulation period, not events (such as the rapture) that occur *prior to* it. Moreover, all of the signs listed in Matthew 24—not just some—must transpire, including "greater anguish than at any time since the world began," along with the sun darkening and the moon giving no light. These events are not taking place in our day, and they *won't* take place until the future tribulation period. Hence, neither these signs nor the parable of the fig tree relate to the rapture, which occurs prior to the tribulation period (John 14:1-3; 1 Thessalonians 1:10; Revelation 3:10). These signs point to the second coming of Christ, which follows the tribulation.

There are other interpreters who suggest that while the parable of the fig tree does indeed relate to tribulation saints, the rapture and the second coming are basically the same event, and hence, for those living in the tribulation period, the parable points to the nearness of the rapture/second coming. (This is posttribulationism—the view that the rapture occurs *after* the tribulation period.) In this view, the church is raptured after the tribulation, and then these raptured believers immediately accompany Christ back down to the earth.

I have some friends who hold to this view. And while I'll always continue to love them as friends, I think they're wrong on this issue. Second Timothy 2:15 instructs that each one of us ought to be a person who "correctly explains the word of truth." The New King James Version translates it "rightly dividing the word of truth." The English Standard Version puts it "rightly handling the word of truth." In my humble opinion, claiming that the rapture and the second coming are the same event fails to rightly divide the word of truth.

Here is why I think this:

1. At the rapture, Christians will meet the Lord in the air, then He will take them to heaven (1 Thessalonians 4:17; John 14:1-3). At the second coming, Christ will descend to the earth and His feet will stand upon the Mount of Olives, which is east of Jerusalem (Zechariah 14:4).

2. The rapture involves Christ coming *for* His people in the air prior to the tribulation period (1 Thessalonians 4:13-17), whereas at the second coming He will bring His people *with* Him to the earth (from heaven) to reign for a thousand years (Revelation 19:11-21; 20:1-6). The fact that Christ comes *with* His people at the second coming presumes He has previously come *for* them.

3. At the rapture, Christ Himself will gather believers out of the world (1 Corinthians 15:52). At the second coming, Christ will send out His angels to gather those who have become believers during the tribulation period (Matthew 24:31).

4. At the rapture, believers will be taken from the earth, while unbelievers will be left behind to go through the seven-year tribulation period (1 Thessalonians 4:13-17; John 14:1-3). At the second coming, by contrast, those who become believers in the Lord during the tribulation period will be left on the earth to enter into Christ's millennial kingdom, while unbelievers will be taken away to punishment (Matthew 24:40-41).

5. Of great relevance to this chapter is the fact there are no prophetic signs that must take place before the rapture can occur. It is a "signless" event. It could happen any moment. That's why we say it is imminent (see Romans 13:11-12; Philippians 4:5; 1 Thessalonians 1:10; Titus 2:13; James 5:8-9; 1 Peter 1:13). This is different from the second coming, which is preceded by seven years' worth of signs during the tribulation period (Revelation 4–18).

Again, then, claiming that the rapture and the second coming are the same event fails to rightly divide the word of truth. In view of such facts, I do not believe the parable of the fig tree points to the rapture.

This Generation Will Not Pass Until...

After enumerating various signs of the times and His parable of the fig tree, Jesus then promised, "I tell you the truth, this generation will not pass from the scene until all these things take place" (Matthew 24:34). I touched on this verse earlier in this book. But I must briefly revisit it here because of its close connection to the parable of the fig tree.

Some have interpreted this prophecy as meaning that because Israel became a nation again in 1948, all the other major prophecies leading up to the second coming of Christ will be fulfilled within a generation of 1948. While that's an intriguing idea, the context of Matthew 24:34 (as well as the entire Olivet Discourse in Matthew

24–25) focuses specifically on the future tribulation period, and not on Israel's rebirth in the year 1948. That being so, the "generation" mentioned in Matthew 24:34 must refer specifically to the future tribulation generation.

There are other interpreters who believe that when Jesus said, "*This generation* will not pass from the scene until all these things take place," He was intending to say that *His* generation would see the fulfillment of all these prophecies. Those who hold to this view are called preterists, and they believe the prophecies in the Olivet Discourse (Matthew 24–25) and most of the prophecies in the book of Revelation were fulfilled in AD 70 when Titus and his Roman warriors overran Jerusalem and its temple.

In my assessment, both of the above views fail to rightly divide the word of truth (2 Timothy 2:15). Contextually, Jesus was saying in this verse that those people who witness the tribulation signs stated earlier in Matthew 24—the sacrilegious object that causes desecration standing in the Holy Place (verse 15), the mass exodus of Jewish people from Jerusalem (verses 16-20), the fact that "there will be greater anguish than at any time since the world began" (verse 21), the rise of "false messiahs and false prophets" (verses 24-27), and the like—will see the coming of Jesus Christ *within that very same generation.* Because it was common knowledge among the Jews that the future tribulation period would last only seven years (Daniel 9:24-27; see also Revelation 12:6,14), it is clear that those who are alive at the beginning of this time will likely still be alive to see the second coming seven years later. The only exception to this would be those who become martyred during this tumultuous time.

The Certainty of the Signs

We've seen that Christ prophesied specific signs that will characterize the tribulation period. These include the rise of false messiahs, wars and threats of wars, nations at war with other nations, famines, earthquakes, persecution, martyrdom, a rise in false prophets, massive deception, rampant sin, the desecration of the Jewish temple, great anguish, a darkened sun, a moon that gives no light, stars falling from the sky, and more. Jesus then taught the parable of the fig tree, by which He said that when one witnesses these signs of the times, one can perceive that His second coming is drawing near.

Christ then pointed to the absolute certainty of the prophetic signs of the times. He affirmed, "Heaven and earth will disappear, but my words will never disappear" (Matthew 24:35). The clear implication is that Christ's prophetic words in the Olivet Discourse will not fail. His prophecies will surely come to pass. His outline of future events can be trusted without hesitation. Everything will happen just as He said it will.

5

Like the Days of Noah

Jesus was a master at speaking in terms His listeners would understand. He often made use of word pictures. In the previous chapter I noted that He sometimes spoke of something in the natural world (planting seeds, a harvest, a vine, and the like) to illustrate a particular truth. In other cases He cited a well-known personality from the Old Testament as a means of illustrating a truth. In His Olivet Discourse, Jesus cited the person of Noah, and the sinful people who lived during his day, as a means of informing His followers of what things will be like during the future tribulation period:

> No one knows the day or hour when these things will happen, not even the angels in heaven or the Son himself. Only the Father knows.
>
> When the Son of Man returns, it will be like it was in Noah's day. In those days before the flood, the people were enjoying banquets and parties and weddings right up to the time Noah entered his boat. People didn't realize what was going to happen until the flood came and swept them all away. That is the way it will be when the Son of Man comes.

Two men will be working together in the field; one will be taken, the other left. Two women will be grinding flour at the mill; one will be taken, the other left.

So you, too, must keep watch! For you don't know what day your Lord is coming (Matthew 24:36-42).

These words are packed with meaning. We'll need to camp here for a while. Let's dig deep so we can appreciate the full significance of what Jesus said.

No One Knows the Day or Hour

Jesus began by affirming that "no one knows the day or hour when these things will happen, not even the angels in heaven or the Son himself. Only the Father knows" (Matthew 24:36). Upon reading these words, two thoughts immediately come to mind: (1) Based on Christ's words, Christians should never set dates for when end-time events occur; and (2) if Jesus does not know the "day or hour" of these events, what does this say about His deity? Let's briefly consider both issues.

Avoid Setting Dates on End-Time Events

If "no one knows the day or hour when these things will happen" except the Father, it is a given that no human being will be able to pinpoint the dates when these prophetic events will unfold. Jesus made this same point following His resurrection and just prior to His ascension into heaven: "When the apostles were with Jesus, they kept asking him, 'Lord, has the time come for you to free Israel and restore our kingdom?' He replied, 'The Father alone has the authority to set those dates and times, and they are not for you to know'" (Acts 1:6-7).

We find an insight on all this in Deuteronomy 29:29: "The LORD our God has secrets known to no one. We are not accountable for them, but we and our children are accountable forever for all that he has revealed to us, so that we may obey all the terms of these instructions." In other words, there are certain things that only God knows. God reveals to us only what we need to know—and this does not include the specific dates of future prophetic events.

In view of Jesus's teachings on the matter, it is unwise to attempt to calculate dates for when specific prophetic events will occur. I can think of some additional reasons that date-setting is unwise:

1. Consider the past. The track record of those who have attached dates to specific end-time events over the past 2,000 years has been 100 percent wrong. The history of date-setting is little more than a history of dashed expectations. Learn a lesson from history!

2. The practice of setting dates to specific end-time events may cause some to make unwise or harmful decisions for their lives. Selling one's possessions and heading for the mountains, purchasing bomb shelters, opting out of college, and leaving family and friends are all destructive actions that can potentially injure one's life.

3. Date-setting may damage a Christian's faith in the Bible when expectations fail to materialize.

4. When people lose confidence in the prophetic portions of Scripture, they may also lose their motivation to live in purity and holiness as they anticipate the Lord's prophesied coming (see Titus 2:12-14). For that to happen would be tragic.

5. Date-setting tends toward sensationalism, and sensationalism is unbefitting to a Bible-believing Christian. Christ calls His followers to live soberly and alertly as they await His coming (Mark 13:32-37).

6. Date-setting can damage the cause of Christ. After all, humanists and atheists enjoy scorning Christians who have put stock in end-time predictions—especially when specific dates have been attached to specific events. Why give "ammo" to the enemies of Christianity?

My friend, it is a certainty that the timing of last-days events is in God's hands alone, and you and I haven't been given the exact details (Acts 1:7). So far as the second coming is concerned, it seems best to live as if Jesus were coming today and yet prepare for the future as if He were not coming for a long time. That way, we are ready for time and eternity. Meanwhile, we can always remain excited when we witness the stage being set for the fulfillment of end-time prophecies in our own day, knowing that each day that passes brings us one day closer to the Lord's coming for us.

Examples of Failed Predictions

To illustrate the critical importance of Jesus's words against setting dates for end-time events, let's consider a few events from church history.

Millennial Shivers

At the turn of the first millennium, people were clearly ignoring Jesus's teachings about not setting dates on end-time events. Consider this account:

> Toward the arrival of the first millennium—December 31, 999 A.D.—so many people in the Christian lands of that time actually thought that the world was coming to an end that they proceeded to act in an unaccustomed fashion. In their dealings with each other they became so brotherly, so charitable, so filled with self-abnegation and love for their neighbor that the true millennium, however briefly, seemed to be at hand.[1]

Another account adds:

> Men forgave their neighbors' debts; people confessed their infidelities and wrongdoings. Farm animals were freed as their owners prepared for the final judgment...The churches were besieged by crowds demanding confession and absolution. Commerce was interrupted. Beggars were

liberally fed by the more fortunate. Prisoners were freed, yet many remained—wishing to expiate their sins before the end. Pilgrims flocked to Jerusalem from Europe. Class differences were forgotten. Slaves were freed.

Nearing December, groups of flagellants roamed the countryside whipping each other.

Christmas passed with a splendid outpouring of love and piety. Food shops gave away food and merchants refused payment. Of course, when December 31st approached a general frenzy reached new heights. In Rome, Pope Sylvester II held midnight mass in the Basilica of St. Peters to a standing-room-only audience. But they weren't standing. All lay on their knees praying.

After the mass had been said, a deathly silence fell. The clock kept on ticking away its last minutes as Pope Sylvester raised his hands to the sky. The attendees at this time lay with their faces to the ground listening to the *tick tick tick*.

Suddenly the clock stopped. Several bodies, stricken by fear, dropped dead as the congregation began screaming in terror. Just as it had suddenly stopped ticking, the clock resumed to meet the midnight hour. Deathly silence still reigned until the clock ticked past 12. Bells in the tower began to scream jubilantly. Pope Sylvester stretched out his hands and gave a blessing over his flock. When the *Te Deum* had been sung, men and women fell in each other's arms, laughing and crying and exchanging the kiss of peace.

Not long after the suspense at St. Peter's and elsewhere, life resumed its normal rhythm. Owners captured their once-freed animals. Merchants ceased giving away their goods. Prisoners were captured to be placed back in the slammer. Debts were remembered. And life went on as if nothing happened.[2]

Did all of this really happen around AD 1000? Some are convinced of it.[3] However, indisputable historical evidence seems lacking.[4] The question boils down to this: If a widespread apocalyptic panic really occurred at the turn of the first millennium, wouldn't we have more than the surviving 12 or 13 accounts of what happened—only half of which mention apocalyptic panic?[5]

Raoul Glaber was a Burgundian monk born in the late tenth century. He wrote *Histories*, a volume considered by many to be a prime source for what happened at the turn of the first millennium. His writings point to a widespread panic concerning the approaching end.[6] A number of historians, however, dispute Glaber's work, suggesting that he perhaps exaggerated things.[7]

The best historical analyses indicate that while there probably was no mass hysteria or panic at the close of the first millennium, there was indeed a widespread serious concern that the end of the world may be drawing near. We find this view reflected in the works of many respectable scholars.

Reformed scholar Louis Berkhof, in his *History of Christian Doctrines*, confirms that

> in the tenth century there was a widespread expectation of the approaching end of the world...It was associated with the idea of the speedy coming of Antichrist. Christian art often chose its themes from eschatology. The hymn *Dies Irae* sounded the terrors of the coming judgment, painters depicted the end of the world on the canvas, and Dante gave a vivid description of hell in his *Divina Commedia*.[8]

Philip Schaff—in his highly respected *History of the Christian Church*—gives a flavor of that era when he writes that Pope Sylvester II (who lived around AD 1000) gave "the first impulse, though prematurely, to the crusades at a time when hundreds of pilgrims flocked to the Holy Land in expectation of the end of the world after the lapse of the first Christian millennium."[9]

Stanley J. Grenz, in his well-received book *The Millennial Maze*, said,

Repeatedly church history has witnessed times of increased speculation concerning the end and the advent of a golden age on earth. The approach of the year A.D. 1000, for example, caused a great stir of expectations. When both that year and A.D. 1033 (a thousand years after Christ's death) passed, interest turned to A.D. 1065, for in that year Good Friday coincided with the Day of the Annunciation. Multitudes journeyed to Jerusalem to await the Lord's return, some arriving already during the previous year and waiting in the Holy City until after Easter.[10]

Grenz also observed that "Augustine's various statements concerning the meaning of the millennium mentioned in Revelation 20 were not without some ambiguity." Indeed, Grenz said,

> They could be (and were) readily understood to indicate that Christ's Second Coming should occur one thousand years after his first advent. This implicit prediction, carrying as it did the authority of the bishop of Hippa coupled both with the theme of the old age of the world and with a rise in political and natural disasters, resulted in a great sense of anticipation in parts of Christendom first as A.D. 1000 and then as A.D. 1033 approached.[11]

In his in-depth study titled *The Year 1000*, Henri Focillon concluded, "We have established that in the middle of the tenth century there existed a movement, a groundswell of the belief that the world was drawing to a close."[12] And "once the terminal year of the millennium has passed, the belief in the end of the world spreads with renewed vigor in the course of the eleventh century."[13] Though properly recognizing this groundswell, Focillon was careful to point out that there was no mass hysteria, as some of the more sensationalistic accounts of the time seem to indicate.

Here is the point I am building up to: Just as many people were concerned about the end of the world around the turn of the first millennium, so there were many who were concerned about the approach of the year AD 2000. Many believed the end of the world was near; others believed a glorious utopia awaited us. At both AD 1000 and AD 2000, date-setting proved fallacious. All of this could have been avoided had these people heeded Jesus's words against setting dates for end-time events.

Edgar C. Whisenant's "88 Reasons"

In early 1988, Edgar C. Whisenant published a book entitled *88 Reasons Why the Rapture Will Be in 1988*. This 58-page work sold a whopping 4.5 million copies and stirred no small controversy in the church. The rapture, Whisenant said, would occur between September 11 and 13 in 1988.

In calculating when the rapture would occur, Whisenant relied on such un-Christian sources as pyramidology, astrology, divination, and numerology.[14] For reasons 64 and 65 in his book, Whisenant relied on the testimony of astrologer-psychic Jeane Dixon.[15]

Amazingly, one preacher planned a 1988 tour of Israel to coincide with Whisenant's date, and mentioned the possibility of being raptured from the Holy Land as a sales incentive. Prospective tourists were enticed by the idea that they might ascend into glory not far from where Jesus Himself ascended into heaven.[16]

As one might expect, when Whisenant's date for the rapture did not pan out, he adjusted his calculations and set forth other dates. He changed the September 11-13 date to October 3, and when that date failed, he declared, "It is going to be in a few weeks anyway." Did Whisenant repent when that date failed? No! Instead, he then claimed his calculations were off by a year and that Christ would return during Rosh Hashanah (September 30) in 1989, or perhaps at the end of the Feast of Tabernacles on October 14-20, 1989.[17] Again, he was wrong. He should have heeded Christ's warning against setting dates.

Rapture Predictions in Korea

A full-page ad appeared in a 1991 *USA Today* newspaper and proclaimed, "RAPTURE: OCTOBER 28, 1992—JESUS IS COMING IN THE AIR." Those who ran the ad also said that on October 28, "50 million people will die in earthquakes, 50 million in traffic accidents, 50 million from fire, 50 million from collapsed buildings, 1.4 billion from World War III, and 1.4 billion from a separate Armageddon."[18]

These messages were sent out by the worldwide Hyoo-go ("Rapture") or Jong Mal Ron ("end-time theory") movement—a "loose connection of Korean sects mixing fanaticism, mysticism, and apocalyptic zeal."[19] At that time, press estimates of the size of this movement ranged from 20,000 to 100,000 people.

As the predicted doomsday drew near, Hyoo-go proponents provoked social upheaval in South Korea. According to one news report, "at least four suicides and several abortions were linked with the movement—the latter because some women were afraid of being 'too heavy' to be caught up to heaven. Numerous secondary and elementary school students abandoned classes. Parents and families of the movement's followers feared that if the Rapture did not take place as predicted there would be a mass suicide."[20]

Finally, the anticipated day arrived. Faithful believers gathered in the church in Seoul, Korea, to await the rapture. A news report documented that "some 1,500 police officers and 200 detectives were posted outside and inside the church in case anyone became violent or attempted suicide. Yet when the appointed hour passed uneventfully, many of the people simply wept. Said one devastated member: 'God lied to us.'"[21]

This illustrates just how far people can go in their apocalyptic zeal. They should have heeded Jesus's words against setting dates.

Harold Camping's 1994 Rapture Prediction

Harold Camping wrote a controversial book titled *1994?*, in which he predicted that Christ would return in September of 1994. "No book ever written is as audacious or bold as one that claims to predict the timing of the end of the world, and that is precisely what this book presumes to do."[22]

Camping warned his followers, "If I am correct in this, and there is every indication that I am, we have a very short time left to get right with God." In the book he claimed that "when September 6, 1994 arrives, no one else can become saved. The end has come."[23] He also claimed that the likelihood of him being wrong about his calculations was "very remote."[24] He warned, "I would be very surprised if the world reaches the year 2000."[25]

Camping's prediction failed *spectacularly*. But he wasn't finished. He later prophesied that Jesus would come for His own on May 21, 2011. Following this, there would allegedly be five months of planet-wide fire, brimstone, and plagues, with millions of people dying each day. The final destruction of the world was to be on October 21, 2011. *Another spectacular failure!*

Still other Christian leaders have taken a stab a date-setting. Prophecy teacher Mary Stewart Relfe said she received "divine revelations from the Lord" indicating that the second coming of Christ would occur in 1997.[26] Lester Sumrall said in his book *I Predict 2000 AD*, "I predict the absolute fullness of man's operation on planet Earth by the year 2000 AD. Then Jesus Christ shall reign from Jerusalem for 1,000 years."[27]

Certainly I believe that Christ calls us to be accurate observers of the times so we can give studied consideration as to whether we may be living in the end times (see Matthew 16:1-3; 24:32-33). The parable of the fig tree urges Christ's tribulation-era followers to be watchful for the signs of the times coming to pass. However, while we can be excited that we may be in the end times, Scripture prohibits dates being set for specific prophetic events. Christ's emphasis remains focused on faithfulness, watchfulness, stewardship, expectancy, and preparedness. Those are the qualities that ought to characterize Christians in the end times.

I strongly suspect that in the coming decades, there will be more date-setters who write books and do radio or TV shows. *Don't be deceived.*

What About Christ's Deity?

If Jesus Himself does not know "the day or hour" of these events, and only the Father knows, what does this say about Jesus's deity? This is a critically important question and deserves a thorough answer.

I can promise you there is indeed a good answer. But it requires that I provide a bit of theological backdrop relating to the incarnation. Though a bit complex, the point I want you to grasp is that the eternal Son of God, prior to the incarnation, was one in person and nature (He had a wholly divine nature). In the incarnation, however, Jesus became *two* in nature (divine and human) while remaining *one* person. The Son, who had already been a person for all eternity past, joined Himself not with a human person but with a human nature at the incarnation. (I know this may seem a bit confusing, but hang with me. I'll clarify my meaning below.)

One of the most complex aspects of the relationship between Christ's two natures is that, while the attributes of one nature are never attributed to the other, the attributes of both natures are properly attributed to His one person. *Here's what I mean:* Christ—as God in human flesh—had at the same moment in time what seem to be contradictory qualities. He was finite yet infinite, weak yet omnipotent, increasing in knowledge yet omniscient, limited to being in one place at one time yet omnipresent. In the incarnation, the person of Christ is the partaker of the attributes of both natures so that whatever may be affirmed of either nature—human or divine—may be affirmed of the one person of Jesus Christ.

Though Christ sometimes operated in the sphere of His humanity and at other times in the sphere of His deity, in all cases, what He did and what He was could be attributed to His one person. Even though Christ in His human nature knew hunger (Luke 4:2), weariness (John 4:6), and the need for sleep (Luke 8:23), in His divine nature He was omniscient (John 2:24), omnipresent (John 1:48), and omnipotent (John 11). All of that was experienced by the one person of the incarnate Christ.

The Gospel accounts clearly show that at different times, Christ operated under the major influence of one or the other of His two natures. Indeed, He operated in the human sphere to the extent that it was necessary for Him to accomplish His earthly purpose as determined in the eternal plan of salvation. At the same time, He operated in the divine sphere to the extent that it was possible during the period of His humiliation on earth (Philippians 2:6-9).

Here is the key point: Both of Christ's natures came into play in many events recorded in the Gospels. For example, Christ's initial approach to the fig tree to pick and eat a fig to relieve His hunger reveals that His human mind was unaware of the tree's condition (Matthew 21:19a). (That is, in His humanity, He did not know from a distance that there was no fruit on that tree.) But then He immediately revealed His divine omnipotence by causing the tree to instantly wither (verse 19b).

On another occasion, Jesus, in His divine omniscience, knew that His friend Lazarus had died, so He set off for Bethany (John 11:11). When Jesus arrived, He asked (in his humanness, without exercising omniscience) where Lazarus had been laid (verse 34). Theologian Robert Reymond notes that as the God-man, Jesus was "simultaneously omniscient as God (in company with the other persons of the Godhead) and ignorant of some things as man (in company with the other persons of the human race)."[28]

All this helps to give a proper understanding of Jesus's comment in Matthew 24:36: "No one knows the day or hour when these things will happen, not even the angels in heaven or the Son himself. Only the Father knows." In this passage, Jesus was speaking from the vantage point of His humanity. As a human being, Jesus was not omniscient, but was limited in understanding just as all humans are. If Jesus had been speaking from the perspective of His divinity, He would not have said the same thing.

Scripture is abundantly clear that in His divine nature, Jesus was omniscient—just as omniscient as the Father. The apostle John said of Jesus that "no one needed to tell him about human nature, for he knew what was in each person's heart" (John 2:25). The disciples said, "Now we understand that you know everything, and there's no need to question you. From this we believe that you came from God" (John 16:30). After the resurrection, when Jesus asked Peter for the third time whether Peter loved Him, the disciple responded, "Lord, you know everything. You know that I love you" (John 21:17).

Bible scholar Thomas Schultz has provided an excellent summary of the abundant evidence for Christ's omniscience:

> First, He knows the inward thoughts and memories of man, an ability peculiar to God (1 Kings 8:39; Jeremiah 17:9-16). He saw the evil in the hearts of the scribes (Matthew 9:4); He knew beforehand those who would reject Him (John 13:11) and those who would follow Him (John 10:14). He could read the hearts of every man and woman (Mark 2:8; John 1:48; 2:24-25; 4:16-19; Acts 1:24; 1 Corinthians 4:5; Revelation 2:18-23). A mere human can no more than make an intelligent guess as to what is in the hearts and minds of others.

Second, Christ has knowledge of other facts beyond the possible comprehension of any man. He knew just where the fish were in the water (Luke 5:4-6; John 21:6-11), and He knew just which fish contained the coin (Matthew 17:27). He knew future events (John 11:11; 18:4), details that would be encountered (Matthew 21:2-4), and He knew that Lazarus had died (John 11:14).

Third, He possessed an inner knowledge of the Godhead showing the closest possible communion with God as well as perfect knowledge. He knows the Father as the Father knows Him (Matthew 11:27; John 7:29; 8:55; 10:15; 17:25).

The fourth and consummating teaching of Scripture along this line is that Christ knows all things (John 16:30; 21:17), and that in Him are hidden all the treasures of wisdom and knowledge (Colossians 2:3).[29]

Certainly a key affirmation of Christ's omniscience is the fact that He hears and answers the prayers of His innumerable people. "When Jesus claimed for Himself the prerogative to hear and to answer the prayers of His disciples," Robert Reymond suggested, "He was claiming omniscience. One who can hear the innumerable prayers of His disciples—offered to Him night and day, day in and day out throughout the centuries—keep each request infallibly related to its petitioner, and answer each one in accordance with the divine mind and will would need Himself to be omniscient."[30]

Now, here's something important to think about: Philippians 2:6-7 says of Jesus that "though he was God, he did not think of equality with God as something to cling to. Instead, he gave up his divine privileges; he took the humble position of a slave and was born as a human being." When our text tells us that Christ "gave up his divine privileges," it means He submitted to a voluntary nonuse of some of His divine attributes *on some occasions* in order to accomplish His messianic objectives. Christ could never have actually surrendered any of His attributes, for then He would have ceased to be God. But He could (and did) voluntarily cease using some of them on occasion during His time on earth (approximately 4 BC to AD 29) in order to live among human beings and their limitations.

To sum up, then, Christ, in His deity, has absolute and undiminished omniscience. He knows all. But in His humanity, Jesus was just as ignorant as any other human. When He became incarnate, there were occasions when He chose not to use His divine attributes. Matthew 24:36 is an example of this. In this verse, Jesus spoke only as a human.

Like the Days of Noah

Following Jesus's exhortation against setting dates for end-time events, He next instructed His followers:

> When the Son of Man returns, it will be like it was in Noah's day. In those days before the flood, the people were enjoying banquets and parties and weddings right up to the time Noah entered his boat. People didn't realize what was going to happen until the flood came and swept them all away. That is the way it will be when the Son of Man comes (Matthew 24:37-39).

This is such a great analogy. The days of Noah were characterized by carousing, partying, and unpreparedness. That's how it will be prior to the second coming of Christ. Just as it was in the days of Noah, people will be engaged in life as usual, having no concept that a judgment is imminent, and that the end is near. Just as Noah had warned the people of his day and was ignored (2 Peter 2:5), so will many people during the tribulation period ignore God's witnesses—including the two prophetic witnesses of Revelation 11 and the 144,000 Jewish witnesses of Revelation 7 and 14. Judgment will fall suddenly and unexpectedly.

If we really want to understand what the days of Noah were like, it is best to consult the book of Genesis, which contains a historical account of Noah and the days in which he lived. This provides a broader context for Jesus's words in the Olivet Discourse.

In Genesis 6:5 we read, "The LORD observed the extent of human wickedness on the earth, and he saw that everything they thought or imagined was consistently and totally evil." The sin of humankind was both extensive and intensive. It was widespread on a global level, and the sins were particularly vile. Humankind had passed a critical threshold of degradation. All the carousing and partying involved unrepentant sin and an utter disregard for responsibility to God.

Notice the reference to "everything they thought or imagined." Sin is first conceived in the mind. It begins in the thought life. As Jeremiah 17:9 puts it, "The human heart is the most deceitful of all things, and desperately wicked. Who really knows how bad it is?" Jesus likewise said that sinful actions emerge from "whatever is in your heart" (Matthew 12:34). He also said, "From within, out of a person's heart, come evil thoughts, sexual immorality, theft, murder, adultery, greed, wickedness, deceit, lustful desires, envy, slander, pride, and foolishness. All these vile things come from within; they are what defile you" (Mark 7:21-23).

The Genesis account then tells us that "the LORD was sorry he had ever made them and put them on the earth. It broke his heart" (Genesis 6:6). The Lord thus resolved to bring judgment upon sinful humankind.

Noah, however, "found favor with the LORD" (Genesis 6:8). Noah was "a righteous man, the only blameless person living on earth at the time, and he walked in close fellowship with God" (verse 9).

In contrast to Noah's righteousness, "God saw that the earth had become corrupt and was filled with violence. God observed all this corruption in the world, for everyone on earth was corrupt"

(Genesis 6:11-12). As a result, God resolved to bring judgment upon the world (verse 13). But Noah and his family were to be rescued from the judgment of the flood (verses 14-22).

It is notable that in the Bible, we often witness sudden judgment falling upon the wicked. For the people living during Noah's time, the flood was sudden and catastrophic. We read in Proverbs 6:15 that the wicked "will be destroyed suddenly, broken in an instant beyond all hope of healing." Proverbs 24:22 says that "disaster will hit them suddenly." Isaiah 47:11 declares that "a catastrophe will strike you suddenly, one for which you are not prepared." God warns in Jeremiah 15:8, "I will cause anguish and terror to come upon them suddenly."

This same kind of suddenness will characterize God's judgment on the world during the tribulation period. People will be unprepared for it. They'll be carousing around, tolerating every form of evil, and oblivious to the reality that judgment is imminent.

While Matthew 24:37-39 refers specifically to the future seven-year tribulation period, we cannot help but notice that the attitudes of carousing around and tolerance toward all forms of evil while utterly disregarding God are pervasive even in our own day.

I am reminded of 2 Timothy 4:3, where the apostle Paul warns, "A time is coming when people will no longer listen to sound and wholesome teaching. They will follow their own desires and will look for teachers who will tell them whatever their itching ears want to hear." We might loosely paraphrase this passage, "A time is coming when people will no longer tolerate sound and wholesome teaching, but they will tolerate teachers who tell them whatever they want to hear."

These words are spoken about the end times, and they characterize Noah's day as well. As it was in Noah's day, so it will be in the end times.

To recap:

- Just as there was great evil in Noah's day, so there will be in the end times.
- Just as there was a lot of carousing around in sin during Noah's day, so there will be during the end times.
- Just as people ignored the preaching of righteousness in Noah's day, so will people do the same in the end times.
- Just as judgment fell suddenly during Noah's day, so will it fall suddenly in the end times.
- Just as people were unprepared for judgment in Noah's day, so will they be unprepared in the end times.
- Just as Noah and his family were rescued in an ark before the judgment of the flood fell, so the church will be rescued via the rapture prior to the beginning of the tribulation period.
- Just as those "left behind" by the ark in Noah's day suffered judgment, so will those left behind after the rapture suffer through the tribulation period.

These are days for discernment. These are days for sober living. These are days to be watchful and ready for what is to come. These are days to rejoice—*for every day that passes brings us one day closer to the rapture!*

6

More Prophetic Parables

Jesus's teachings take a variety of forms, but a full third of them involve the use of parables. We've already examined one such parable—that of the fig tree.

The word *parable* means "a placing alongside of" for the purpose of comparison. A parable is a teaching tool. Jesus often told stories from real life—involving, for example, a woman who lost a coin, or a shepherd watching over sheep, or a worker in a vineyard—and used those stories to illustrate spiritual truths. By taking such stories and placing them alongside spiritual truths, the process of comparison helps us to understand Jesus's spiritual teachings more clearly.

A number of Jesus's parables teach important prophetic truths about the nature of the kingdom from the time of Christ up through the end times. This shows us that Christ's prophetic foresight encompasses all of human history, and not merely the distant last days.

Other parables have specific reference to the tribulation period—that future seven-year period during which the wrath of God will fall upon the sinful world. These parables typically stress the need for readiness and watchfulness regarding the Lord's coming.

Two of Jesus's parables relate to what takes place among believers *following* the tribulation period. Through these parables, Jesus teaches that those who serve Him faithfully during earthly life will be rewarded in the millennial kingdom and the eternal state that follows.

Before examining specific parables, let's first briefly address the controversial matter as to why Jesus—by His own words—communicated truth through parables *only to certain people*, and not to all. In Matthew 13:10-11, we read that "his disciples came and asked him, 'Why do you use parables when you talk to the people?' He replied, 'You are permitted to understand the secrets of the Kingdom of Heaven, but others are not.'"

A look at the context helps us to understand why Jesus chose to teach this way. In Matthew 13, Jesus is portrayed as being in front of a mixed multitude comprised of both believers and unbelievers. He did not attempt to separate them and then instruct only the believers. Rather, He constructed His teaching so that believers would understand what He said, and unbelievers would not. He did this by using parables.

In Matthew 13:11, the word "secrets" means "mystery." A mystery in the biblical sense is a truth that cannot be discerned merely by human investigation, but requires special revelation from God. Generally this word refers to a truth that was unknown to people living in Old Testament times, but is now revealed to humankind by God (Matthew 13:17; Colossians 1:26). In Matthew 13, Jesus provides information about the kingdom of heaven that had never been revealed before.

However, hardened unbelievers who had willfully and persistently refused Jesus's previous teachings were prevented from understanding these parables. Jesus was apparently following an injunction He provided earlier in the Sermon on the Mount:

"Don't waste what is holy on people who are unholy. Don't throw your pearls to pigs! They will trample the pearls, then turn and attack you" (Matthew 7:6). In other words, don't share these precious truths with those who—because of their open and sometimes violent antagonism toward God—will only show disdain and contempt toward them.

Yet there may also be an element of grace in Christ's actions. For it is possible that He may have prevented unbelievers from understanding the parables because He did not want to add more responsibility to them by imparting new truth for which they would be held responsible at the future judgment.

That said, let's now briefly explore the prophetic teachings contained in some of Jesus's key parables—teachings that Jesus desires all of His followers to know.

Parables Pertaining to the Value and Growth of the Kingdom

The Parable of the Great Feast

In Matthew 22:1-14, Jesus taught His followers a rather long parable of the feast. He affirmed that the kingdom of heaven can be compared to a king who was giving a wedding feast for his son (verses 1-2). When the king invited the guests, they were either indifferent to the request or they mistreated and killed the slave who had delivered the invitation (verses 3-6). The king subsequently punished the murderers (verse 7).

Following this, the king commanded that his slaves go out and find anyone who was willing to come to the feast (Matthew 22:8-10). Those who chose to come were expected to prepare properly by putting on wedding clothes that would be supplied by the king's servants. When the king himself arrived at the feast, he found one man who was not properly attired and commanded him to be cast into punishment (verses 11-13). It is at this point that Jesus said, "Many are called, but few are chosen" (verse 14).

Some elements of this parable may seem confusing to you. Even Bible expositors have different opinions about its meaning. But here's what appears to make the most sense: Jesus taught that the King (Jesus) and His kingdom had been offered to the nation of Israel, but the Jews were indifferent to the offer. The Jews even murdered those who delivered the message—the prophets throughout Old Testament times.

The invitation was then broadened to include "everyone you see"—including the Gentiles. It may be that metaphorically, the wedding garments refer to the righteousness of Christ, which adorns all who trust in Him for salvation (compare with Romans 13:14). Individual responsibility is seen in the parable because people who come to the feast are responsible to put on the garments—perhaps meaning that people are responsible to trust in Christ for salvation. All who reject Christ (refusing to put on the proper clothes, or the righteousness of Christ) will be cast out into punishment. The invitation to salvation is sent out to many people—Jews *and* Gentiles—but comparatively few accept the invitation.

A powerful lesson we learn from this passage is that from the time of Christ up through the last days, the gospel is for both Gentiles and Jews. All are invited, though not all will respond.

The Parable of the Wheat and Weeds

In Matthew 13:24-30, Jesus said,

> The Kingdom of Heaven is like a farmer who planted good seed in his field. But that night as the workers slept, his enemy came and planted weeds among the wheat, then slipped away. When the crop began to grow and produce grain, the weeds also grew.

The farmer's workers went to him and said, "Sir, the field where you planted that good seed is full of weeds! Where did they come from?"

"An enemy has done this!" the farmer exclaimed.

"Should we pull out the weeds?" they asked.

"No," he replied, "you'll uproot the wheat if you do. Let both grow together until the harvest. Then I will tell the harvesters to sort out the weeds, tie them into bundles, and burn them, and to put the wheat in the barn."

Jesus Himself later told the disciples the meaning of this parable:

The Son of Man is the farmer who plants the good seed. The field is the world, and the good seed represents the people of the Kingdom. The weeds are the people who belong to the evil one. The enemy who planted the weeds among the wheat is the devil. The harvest is the end of the world, and the harvesters are the angels.

Just as the weeds are sorted out and burned in the fire, so it will be at the end of the world. The Son of Man will send his angels, and they will remove from his Kingdom everything that causes sin and all who do evil. And the angels will throw them into the fiery furnace, where there will be weeping and gnashing of teeth. Then the righteous will shine like the sun in their Father's Kingdom. Anyone with ears to hear should listen and understand!

This parable clearly teaches that good and evil—*true believers and false believers*—will coexist in the world, mingling together, right up till the time of the final judgment. Then they will be separated.

The Parable of the Growing Seed

Referring again to seeds, Jesus taught another spiritual truth in Mark 4:26-29. He said,

The Kingdom of God is like a farmer who scatters seed on the ground. Night and day, while he's asleep or awake, the seed sprouts and grows, but he does not understand how it happens. The earth produces the crops on its own. First a leaf blade pushes through, then the heads of wheat are formed, and finally the grain ripens. And as soon as the grain is ready, the farmer comes and harvests it with a sickle, for the harvest time has come.

The meaning of the parable is that the fruit that results from sowing a seed—in this case, the "seed" of the Word of God—depends not on the one doing the sowing, but on the life that is in the seed itself (God's supernatural Word). Because 11 of the disciples would soon be commissioned to proclaim Christ's message to the ends of the earth (Matthew 28:19-20), they might fall into the trap of assuming that the harvest of souls depended solely on their efforts. Christ thus wanted to make it clear in this parable that any harvest produced would be the result of sowing the seed and then allowing the life in that seed to manifest itself by growth and fruit at the time of the harvest.

In other words, the Word of God, if faithfully sown, will supernaturally produce its own results. The disciples were simply responsible for doing the sowing. The harvest was in God's hands. The growth of God's kingdom is the result not of the disciples' efforts, but rather, the supernatural nature of God's Word.

The same is true for you and me. As we continue to sow the Word of God among people, it is the supernatural power intrinsic to God's Word that brings results, not our gospel-sharing prowess.

The Parable of the Mustard Seed

In Matthew 13:31-32, Jesus said, "The Kingdom of Heaven is like a mustard seed planted in a field. It is the smallest of all seeds, but it becomes the largest of garden plants; it grows into a tree, and birds come and make nests in its branches."

In this parable, Jesus taught that the kingdom of heaven would have an almost imperceptible beginning. The kingdom was small back in the days of Christ and His followers. But just as a small mustard seed can produce a large plant—it can grow up past 15 feet high—so the kingdom would start small but grow to be very large. By the time of Christ's second coming, the kingdom would encompass believers all over the world.

The Parable of the Yeast

In Matthew 13:33, Jesus said, "The Kingdom of Heaven is like the yeast a woman used in making bread. Even though she put only a little yeast in three measures of flour, it permeated every part of the dough." Scholars have different opinions about what Jesus was saying here. Some argue that because yeast sometimes represents evil elsewhere in Scripture (Matthew 16:12; Mark 8:15; Luke 12:1; 1 Corinthians 5:6-8; Galatians 5:9), Jesus was saying that evil will be present in some form within Christendom up until Christ comes again (see 1 Timothy 4:1-5). Perhaps, then, it may refer to the many people who profess to be Christians without having genuine faith.

Other scholars suggest it would be wrong to assume that simply because yeast represents evil in other verses that it must represent evil in the present context of Matthew 13. Indeed, perhaps yeast was being used in a good sense in this context so that it represents the dynamic growth of the kingdom of God as a result of the penetrating power of the gospel of Christ and the supernatural work of the Holy Spirit.

To expand on this meaning, note that when leaven is introduced into baking flour, a process begins that is steady, continuous, and irreversible. With that in mind, the present parable may be intended to teach that the gospel of Christ, combined with the supernatural power of the Holy Spirit, yields a process that is steady, continuous, and irreversible. Hence, the parable may be pointing to the continued growth of the kingdom of heaven.

I believe this second interpretative option makes the better sense.

The Parables of the Hidden Treasure and the Pearl

In Matthew 13:44-46, Jesus said,

> The Kingdom of Heaven is like a treasure that a man discovered hidden in a field. In his excitement, he hid it again and sold everything he owned to get enough money to buy the field.
>
> Again, the Kingdom of Heaven is like a merchant on the lookout for choice pearls. When he discovered a pearl of great value, he sold everything he owned and bought it!

In these two parables, Jesus was simply pointing to the incredible value of the kingdom of heaven. Those who truly see its importance—regardless of what era of history they live in—will do anything within their power to possess it. They will allow nothing to stand in their way.

To clarify, these parables *should not* be taken to mean that a person could buy his or her way into the kingdom of heaven by material wealth. Such a conclusion would violate the intent of the parables. In context, the parables simply point to the incalculable value of the kingdom, and that one should be willing to give up everything to attain it. It is the highest of priorities.

The Parable of the Fishing Net

In Matthew 13:47-50, Jesus said,

> The Kingdom of Heaven is like a fishing net that was thrown into the water and caught fish of every kind.

When the net was full, they dragged it up onto the shore, sat down, and sorted the good fish into crates, but threw the bad ones away. That is the way it will be at the end of the world. The angels will come and separate the wicked people from the righteous, throwing the wicked into the fiery furnace, where there will be weeping and gnashing of teeth.

Many scholars believe that in this passage, Jesus was emphasizing that up until His second coming, both genuine and phony (professing) Christians will coexist within the kingdom. At the end of the age, there will be a separation of the righteous from the unrighteous. The righteous—that is, true believers—will be invited into Christ's millennial kingdom, whereas the unrighteous—who profess to be believers but aren't—will be excluded from His kingdom and sent to a place of suffering.

Fishermen can attest that when a net is brought up out of the water, it has all kinds of fish in it—some of them good and worth keeping, and others that are utterly useless. That's why the fishermen separate the fish, keeping only the good and throwing away the bad. At the end of the age, Christ will separate the good from the bad, the true Christians from the phonies, the righteous from the unrighteous.

Parables Relating to the Tribulation Period

The Parable of the Fig Tree

The parable of the fig tree is so significant that earlier I dedicated an entire chapter to discussing its significance (see chapter 4). I will not repeat all that material here, but I will summarize the main point of the parable for the sake of continuity in this chapter.

You'll notice that in chapter 4 I cited Matthew's account of the parable of the fig tree. Here I will cite Luke's account, for he adds a few details not found in Matthew: "Notice the fig tree, or any other tree. When the leaves come out, you know without being told that summer is near. In the same way, when you see all these things taking place, you can know that the Kingdom of God is near" (Luke 21:29-31).

Jesus's point is that when leaves grow on a tree in the spring, it is a sure sign that summer is near. Likewise, when one witnesses the signs mentioned previously in the Olivet Discourse, one can perceive that Christ's coming is drawing near. These signs include the rise of false messiahs, wars and threats of wars, nations at war with other nations, famines, earthquakes, persecution, martyrdom, a rise in false prophets, massive deception, rampant sin, the desecration of the Jewish temple, great anguish, a darkened sun, a moon that gives no light, and stars falling from the sky.

Shortly after the parable of the fig tree, Jesus urged,

> Watch out! Don't let your hearts be dulled by carousing and drunkenness, and by the worries of this life. Don't let that day catch you unaware, like a trap. For that day will come upon everyone living on the earth. Keep alert at all times. And pray that you might be strong enough to escape these coming horrors and stand before the Son of Man (Luke 21:34-36).

We might paraphrase Jesus's words this way:

> These horrific events of the tribulation period will take many people by surprise and lead to great anxiety in their hearts. They will try to numb this anxiety by getting drunk. You, however, should not be taken by surprise, for I have warned you in advance that these things will happen. Therefore, take the parable of the fig tree to heart. Watch and be ready. Do not succumb to debilitating anxiety or drunkenness. Instead, keep your eyes focused on the fact that I am indeed coming soon. Pray that you may escape being sidetracked like so many others during this

time who will be paralyzed by fear. Do not have "double vision," with one eye on me and the other eye on the anxieties of the tribulation period. Maintain "single vision" and keep your focus on me. Then when I do come, you will be ready.

Parable of the Faithful Servant

In Matthew 24:45-51, Jesus said,

> A faithful, sensible servant is one to whom the master can give the responsibility of managing his other household servants and feeding them. If the master returns and finds that the servant has done a good job, there will be a reward. I tell you the truth, the master will put that servant in charge of all he owns. But what if the servant is evil and thinks, "My master won't be back for a while," and he begins beating the other servants, partying, and getting drunk? The master will return unannounced and unexpected, and he will cut the servant to pieces and assign him a place with the hypocrites. In that place there will be weeping and gnashing of teeth.

In this parable, Jesus likens an individual follower or disciple to a servant who has been put in charge of his master's household. Jesus contrasts two possible ways that each professed disciple can carry out the assigned task—faithfully or unfaithfully. Each respective servant has the potential to be faithful or unfaithful with regard to his duties.

The servant who chooses to be faithful conscientiously fulfills his obligations while his master is away. He honors the stewardship entrusted to him. He pays careful attention to the details of his assigned task, and seeks to avoid living carelessly and becoming lax. He so governs his life that he will be prepared whenever his master returns.

By contrast, the servant who chooses to be unfaithful calculates that his master will be away for a long time and hence decides to mistreat his fellow servants and "live it up" himself. He lives carelessly, callously, and self-indulgently, and does not fulfill his responsibilities. It is clear that he is a servant in name only—*a hypocrite*. He is not a true servant.

Now, we recall that the entire Olivet Discourse in Matthew 24–25 focuses on the tribulation period. Contextually, then, this parable indicates that during the tribulation period, those who profess to serve Christ must make a pivotal choice: be faithful servants, doing the Lord's will at all times, or be unfaithful servants, neglecting God's will and living self-indulgently. Those who are faithful will be rewarded at the Lord's return, entering into His millennial kingdom. Those who are unfaithful will be punished at the Lord's return and excluded from His millennial kingdom.

The Parable of the Ten Bridesmaids

In Matthew 25:1-13, Jesus said,

> The Kingdom of Heaven will be like ten bridesmaids who took their lamps and went to meet the bridegroom. Five of them were foolish, and five were wise. The five who were foolish didn't take enough olive oil for their lamps, but the other five were wise enough to take along extra oil. When the bridegroom was delayed, they all became drowsy and fell asleep.
>
> At midnight they were roused by the shout, "Look, the bridegroom is coming! Come out and meet him!"
>
> All the bridesmaids got up and prepared their lamps. Then the five foolish ones asked the others, "Please give us some of your oil because our lamps are going out."
>
> But the others replied, "We don't have enough for all of us. Go to a shop and buy some for yourselves."
>
> But while they were gone to buy oil, the bridegroom

came. Then those who were ready went in with him to the
marriage feast, and the door was locked. Later, when the
other five bridesmaids returned, they stood outside, calling, "Lord! Lord! Open the door for us!"

But he called back, "Believe me, I don't know you!"

So you, too, must keep watch! For you do not know the
day or hour of my return.

Contextually, this parable refers to true believers who are living
during the future tribulation period, prior to the second coming of
Christ. (Again, keep in mind that Christ's entire Olivet Discourse
in Matthew 24–25 addresses events that transpire during the tribulation period.) The parable teaches that Jesus's coming will be sudden, when it is not expected. Believers are those who anticipate His
coming and seek to be prepared for it, living their lives accordingly.
His return will terminate the opportunity for people to "prepare
themselves" (trust in Jesus) to enter His kingdom. Only those who
are already prepared (saved by trusting in Christ) will be permitted
to enter. No unprepared (unsaved) person will be permitted to enter.

Parables Pertaining to the Millennial Kingdom and the Eternal State

The Parable of the Talents

In Matthew 25:14-30, Jesus said that

the Kingdom of Heaven can be illustrated by the story of
a man going on a long trip. He called together his servants
and entrusted his money to them while he was gone. He
gave five bags of silver to one, two bags of silver to another,
and one bag of silver to the last—dividing it in proportion
to their abilities. He then left on his trip.

The servant who was given five bags of silver invested it and made
a good return on the money. To this servant the master said: "Well

done, my good and faithful servant. You have been faithful in handling this small amount, so now I will give you many more responsibilities. Let's celebrate together!" (verse 21).

The servant who was given two bags of silver invested it and made a good return on the money. To this servant the master said: "Well done, my good and faithful servant. You have been faithful in handling this small amount, so now I will give you many more responsibilities. Let's celebrate together!" (verse 23).

But to the servant who was given one bag of silver, who did nothing with it, the master had nothing but harsh words of judgment. The bag of silver was withdrawn from him.

We then come to the life lesson Jesus wanted to teach: "To those who use well what they are given, even more will be given, and they will have an abundance. But from those who do nothing, even what little they have will be taken away." A number of Bible expositors believe that when Jesus said, "To those who use well what they are given, even more will be given, and they will have an abundance," He had in mind giving these faithful believers greater responsibilities during the millennial kingdom and the eternal state that follows.

The Parable of the Ten Servants

In Luke 19:11-26, Jesus told a rather long parable to communicate that our service assignments in the millennial kingdom and the eternal state will relate to how faithfully we serve God during our mortal lives on earth. In the parable, various servants rendered varying levels of faithfulness to their master. To the faithful servant, the master said, "You have been faithful with the little I entrusted to you, so you will be governor of ten cities as your reward" (verse 17).

The idea seems to be that the more faithful we are in serving God in the present life, the more we will be entrusted with in the millennial kingdom and the eternal state with regard to our service to

God. Conversely, the less faithful we are in serving God in the present life, the less we will be entrusted with.

This has rather profound implications for the way we live today. Faithfulness *in the now* is a preparation for great blessing *later*.

What We Learn from the Parables

We have seen in this chapter that Christ has provided a number of prophetic insights about the future in the form of parables. To help you see the big picture, I've summarized the parables below:

The Parable of the Great Feast—God offered the kingdom to Israel, but the Jews were indifferent to the offer. God's message of the kingdom is now for all people, including the Gentiles.

The Parable of the Wheat and Weeds—True and false believers will coexist and mingle together until the future judgment, when they will be separated.

The Parable of the Growing Seed—The Word of God, if faithfully sown, will supernaturally produce its own results, and does not depend on the one doing the sowing.

The Parable of the Mustard Seed—The kingdom started small, but it will grow immeasurably large.

The Parable of the Yeast—There will be a continued growth and expansion of the kingdom throughout church history.

The Parables of the Hidden Treasure and the Pearl—The kingdom has incalculable value.

The Parable of the Fishing Net—Up until Christ's second coming, when judgment will take place, there will be both genuine and phony (professing) Christians who coexist within the kingdom.

The Parable of the Fig Tree—Jesus urged His followers to seek to be accurate observers of the times so that when the "signs of the times" come to pass, they will recognize them and live in preparedness for the Lord's coming.

Parable of the Faithful Servant—Those who profess to serve Christ during the tribulation period must make a crucial choice: be faithful servants, doing the Lord's will at all times, or be unfaithful servants, neglecting God's will and living self-indulgently.

The Parable of the Ten Bridesmaids—Believers are to anticipate the Lord's coming and be prepared for it, living their lives accordingly.

The Parable of the Talents and *The Parable of the Ten Servants*— The more faithful we are in serving God in the present life, the more we will be entrusted with in the next life, the millennial kingdom, and the eternal state.

In the next chapter, we will focus attention on Jesus's teachings about His second coming.

7

The Second Coming of Jesus Christ

The second coming is that resplendently glorious event when Jesus Christ—the King of kings and Lord of lords—will return to the earth at the end of the present age and set up His kingdom. The very same Jesus who ascended into heaven will physically and visibly come again at the second coming (Acts 1:9-11).

A rather awe-inspiring description of the second coming is found in Revelation 19:11-16:

> I saw heaven opened, and a white horse was standing there. Its rider was named Faithful and True, for he judges fairly and wages a righteous war. His eyes were like flames of fire, and on his head were many crowns. A name was written on him that no one understood except himself. He wore a robe dipped in blood, and his title was the Word of God. The armies of heaven, dressed in the finest of pure white linen, followed him on white horses. From his mouth came a sharp sword to strike down the nations. He will rule them with an iron rod. He will release the fierce wrath of God, the Almighty, like juice flowing from a winepress. On his robe at his thigh was written this title: King of all kings and Lord of all lords.

Let's not forget that even though the apostle John wrote these words, the entire book of Revelation was "a revelation from Jesus Christ" that was passed on "to his servant John" (Revelation 1:1). So Christ is the ultimate source of this revelation about the second coming. And this revelation is rich with meaning.

In Bible times, generals in the Roman army rode white horses. Christ, the glorious Commander-in-Chief of the armies of heaven, will ride a white horse, which will signify His coming in triumph over the forces of wickedness in the world. This is in noted contrast to the lowly colt upon which Jesus rode during His first coming (see Zechariah 9:9).

Our text tells us that "on his head were many crowns" (Revelation 19:12). These represent Christ's total sovereignty and royal kingship. No one will be in a position to challenge His kingly authority.

Jesus is called "King of all kings and Lord of all lords" (Revelation 19:16). This title means that Jesus is absolutely supreme and sovereign over all earthly rulers and angelic powers (1 Timothy 6:15; see also Deuteronomy 10:17; Psalm 136:3). The long-awaited messianic King has now finally arrived.

Unpreparedness, Watchfulness, and Readiness

Christ spoke much more directly about the second coming in His Olivet Discourse. While He addressed various aspects of His second coming in this sermon, I find it intriguing that He devoted so much of His message to how people in the world will be woefully unprepared for His return. A consistent emphasis is how His people must be watchful and ready for His coming.

In one part of the sermon, which I addressed in chapter 5, Jesus compared peoples' unpreparedness for His return to peoples' unpreparedness for the flood back in Noah's day. Consider His words: "When the Son of Man returns, it will be like it was in Noah's day. In those days before the flood, the people were enjoying banquets and parties and weddings right up to the time Noah entered his boat. People didn't realize what was going to happen until the flood came and swept them all away. That is the way it will be when the Son of Man comes" (Matthew 24:39-40).

Jesus then stressed the need for watchfulness and readiness among His own people:

> So you, too, must keep watch! For you don't know what day your Lord is coming. Understand this: If a homeowner knew exactly when a burglar was coming, he would keep watch and not permit his house to be broken into. You also must be ready all the time, for the Son of Man will come when least expected (Matthew 24:41-44).

Jesus continued to emphasize similar points throughout the rest of the sermon:

- "As the lightning flashes in the east and shines to the west, so it will be when the Son of Man comes" (Matthew 24:27). A lightning flash is sudden and unexpected.
- "You, too, must keep watch! For you don't know what day your Lord is coming...You also must be ready all the time, for the Son of Man will come when least expected" (Matthew 24:42,44). (Note that the Greek word translated "keep watch" can also be rendered "keep alert.")
- "You, too, must keep watch! For you do not know the day or hour of my return" (Matthew 25:13).

Later in the book of Revelation, Jesus urged, "Look, I will come as unexpectedly as a thief! Blessed are all who are watching for me, who keep their clothing ready so they will not have to walk around naked and ashamed" (Revelation 16:15).

As we peruse Christ's prophetic words of urgency, there are four observations we can make:

1. When Jesus repeats a point a number of times, we must assume it is important. Because Jesus repeatedly warned against unpreparedness and exhorted His people to watchfulness and readiness, His people must respond with the same sense of urgency that characterized Christ's prophetic warning.

2. Because Jesus's words about watchfulness and readiness are in His Olivet Discourse, a sermon that focuses on the future tribulation period, these exhortations to readiness are specifically applicable to those who become believers during the tribulation period. (Remember that Christians will have already been raptured prior to the beginning of the tribulation period—John 14:1-3; 1 Corinthians 15:50-52; 1 Thessalonians 4:13-18. But many will become believers during the tribulation, as Revelation 7:9-17 affirms.)

3. The tribulation period will involve great suffering for people worldwide. There will be good reason for constant discouragement and despair. In the midst of such darkness, the efforts of God's people to remain watchful and ready for Christ's return keeps their faith alive and their hope strong.

4. Christ's exhortations to watchfulness and readiness for His coming seem closely connected to His concern about a lack of faith when He returns: "When the Son of Man returns, how many will he find on the earth who have faith?" (Luke 18:8). It's likely that Jesus strategically asked the question about finding faith on earth to spur His own followers on to faithfulness. Elsewhere in prophetic Scripture we learn that in the end times, many will fall away from the faith (see 2 Thessalonians 2:3-4; 1 Timothy 4:1; 2 Timothy 4:3-4). But Jesus did not want this to happen to His followers. Hence, He apparently asked the question to motivate faith and commitment. Jesus continued to urge people on to faithfulness throughout the rest of Luke (21:8-19,34-36; 22:31-32,40,46).

In short, *keep the faith, be watchful, be ready*!

The Sign of the Son of Man

As Christ continued to deliver His Olivet Discourse, He said, "At last, the sign that the Son of Man is coming will appear in the heavens, and there will be deep mourning among all the peoples of the earth. And they will see the Son of Man coming on the clouds of heaven with power and great glory" (Matthew 24:30).

Christ's reference to Himself as the "Son of Man" reminds us of the Old Testament prophet Daniel, who, in a vision, witnessed "someone like a son of man" (Daniel 7:13). In Daniel's vision, the Son of Man "approached the Ancient One and was led into his presence. He was given authority, honor, and sovereignty over all the nations of the world, so that people of every race and nation and language would obey him. His rule is eternal—it will never end. His kingdom will never be destroyed" (Daniel 7:13-14).

"The Ancient One" is the Father, the first person of the Trinity. "Son of Man" is a messianic title of Jesus Christ, the second person of the Trinity (see Matthew 24:30; 25:31; 26:24; Mark 13:26; Luke 21:27; John 12:34). In Daniel's vision, the second person of the Trinity appears before the first person. Jesus, the divine Messiah, appears before the heavenly Father. Scripture consistently portrays Jesus in submission to the heavenly Father: "I have come down from heaven to do the will of God who sent me, not to do my own will" (John 6:38; see also John 4:34; 5:19; 14:31; 16:28). In Daniel's vision, we witness the Father giving Jesus, the Son of Man, supreme authority.

The term "Son of Man" is commonly ascribed to Christ throughout the Gospels (Matthew 8:20; 20:18; 24:30). The title is often used in the context of Christ's deity. For example, the Bible says that only God can forgive sins (Isaiah 43:25; Mark 2:7). But Jesus, as the Son of Man, had the power to forgive sins (Mark 2:10).

Now, as noted earlier, after the tribulation period, "the sign that the Son of Man is coming will appear in the heavens, and there will be deep mourning among all the peoples of the earth" (Matthew 24:30). What is "the sign" referenced here? This is an issue of debate among Bible expositors. Some suggest the sign of the cross will appear in the sky for all to see. Others suggest it refers to the lightning that "flashes in the east and shines to the west" (Matthew 24:27). Others suggest that perhaps it is the glory of Christ that will be greatly manifest at the second coming. Still others choose not to define the sign, affirming that the main thing is that Christ Himself will return visibly. Indeed, it may be that the Son of Man Himself is the sign (see Daniel 7:13; Acts 1:11; Revelation 19:11-21).

Whatever the case, the Son of Man will come on the "clouds of heaven" (Matthew 24:30). Clouds are often used in association with God's visible glory (Exodus 16:10; 40:34-35; 1 Kings 8:10-11; Matthew 17:5; 24:30; 26:64). Just as Christ was received by a cloud at His ascension (Acts 1:9), so will He return in the clouds of heaven (Matthew 24:30; 26:64; Mark 13:26; 14:62; Luke 21:27). Just as Jesus left with a visible manifestation of the glory of God (clouds were present), so will He return at the second coming with a visible manifestation of the glory of God (clouds will be present).

Some wonder why there will be "deep mourning among all the peoples of the earth" when Christ comes in glory (Matthew 24:30). There may be a couple of different aspects of this mourning. On the one hand, just prior to the second coming, the Jewish remnant—now living in the wilderness—will finally come to see that Jesus is indeed the divine Messiah, and these Jews will finally trust in Christ for salvation. These will mourn over their previous rejection of the Messiah (see Zechariah 12:10-12). On the other hand, people worldwide who have been living in open defiance and rebellion against God throughout the tribulation period will mourn because they recognize that the divine Judge is now here, and it's time to face the consequences of their rebellion.

The Role of Angels at the Second Coming

Scripture consistently affirms that when Christ visibly and physically returns to earth, a vast host of angels will accompany Him (Revelation 19:14). Jesus prophesied that "the Son of Man will come with his angels in the glory of his Father" (Matthew 16:27). He also prophesied, "When the Son of Man comes in his glory, and all the angels with him, then he will sit upon his glorious throne" (Matthew 25:31). Second Thessalonians 1:7 tells us that Christ "will come with his mighty angels." What a resplendently glorious scene this will be!

Following the second coming, angels will gather people from around the world. In Matthew 24:31, Jesus said, "He will send out his angels with the mighty blast of a trumpet, and they will gather his chosen ones from all over the world—from the farthest ends of the earth and heaven." His "chosen ones" are people who become believers during the tribulation period, and have been scattered throughout the world because of persecution (Matthew 24:16).[1] They are gathered because they are about to be invited to enter into Christ's millennial kingdom—that 1,000-year kingdom on earth—during which Christ will rule on earth from the throne of David.

The angels will also be involved in gathering the wicked: "The Son of Man will send his angels, and they will remove from his Kingdom everything that causes sin and all who do evil. And the angels will throw them into the fiery furnace, where there will be weeping and gnashing of teeth" (Matthew 13:41-42). As if to emphasize His point, Jesus reiterated, "The angels will come and separate the wicked people from the righteous, throwing the wicked into the fiery furnace, where there will be weeping and gnashing of teeth" (Matthew 13:49-50). When Jesus says something twice, it's important.

Christ Will Sit upon a Throne

As Jesus continued His Olivet Discourse, He affirmed that when He comes in glory, "he will sit upon his glorious throne" (Matthew 25:31). The kingship of Jesus Christ is a common theme in Scripture. Genesis 49:10 prophesied that the Messiah would come from the tribe of Judah and reign as a king. In Psalm 2:6, God the Father announced the installation of God the Son as King in Jerusalem. Psalm 110 affirms that the Messiah will subjugate His enemies and rule over them. Daniel 7:13-14 tells us that the Messiah-King will have an everlasting dominion.

In the context of Matthew 25:31, Jesus will sit upon a throne in order to judge the nations (more on this in chapter 8). The nations are comprised of the sheep and the goats, representing the saved and the lost among the Gentiles. According to Matthew 25:32, they will be intermingled and require separation by a special judgment. This judgment follows the second coming, since it occurs "when the Son of Man comes in his glory, and all the angels with him" (Matthew 25:31).

The basis of judgment is how these people treated Christ's "brothers" (Matthew 25:40)—apparently the 144,000 Jewish men who witness to the nations during the seven-year tribulation period (Revelation 7; 14). Those who treat the brothers well (thereby indicating they are Christians, the sheep) will be invited into Christ's millennial kingdom. Those who do not treat the brothers well (thereby indicating they are unbelievers, the goats) will be sent to eternal punishment (Matthew 25:31-46).

Of course, Christ's enthronement extends far beyond the judgment of the nations. Indeed, God promised David that one of his descendants would rule forever on his throne (2 Samuel 7:12-13; 22:51). Like the land promise to Abraham and his descendants, God's promise to David is an unconditional covenant. It did not depend on David in any way for its fulfillment. David realized this when he received the promise from God, and he responded with humility and a recognition of God's sovereignty over human affairs.

The Davidic covenant finds its ultimate fulfillment in Jesus Christ, who was born from the line of David (Matthew 1:1). In the millennial kingdom, He will rule from the throne of David in Jerusalem (Micah 4:1-5; Zephaniah 3:14-20; Zechariah 14). This reign of Christ during the millennial kingdom will extend beyond the Jews to include the Gentile nations as well. Multiple prophecies in Scripture point to Christ's reign during the millennial kingdom:

- "May he reign from sea to sea, and from the Euphrates River to the ends of the earth" (Psalm 72:8).

- "Your king will bring peace to the nations. His realm will stretch from sea to sea and from the Euphrates River to the ends of the earth" (Zechariah 9:10).

- "For a child is born to us, a son is given to us. The government will rest on his shoulders. And he will be called: Wonderful Counselor, Mighty God, Everlasting Father, Prince of Peace. His government and its peace will never end. He will rule with fairness and justice from the throne of his ancestor David for all eternity. The passionate commitment of the Lord of Heaven's Armies will make this happen!" (Isaiah 9:6-7).

- Daniel said, "As my vision continued that night, I saw someone like a son of man coming with the clouds of heaven. He approached the Ancient One and was led into his presence. He was given authority, honor, and sovereignty over all the nations of the world, so that people of every race and nation and language would obey him. His rule is eternal—it will never end. His kingdom will never be destroyed" (Daniel 7:13-14).

Note also that when the angel Gabriel appeared to the young virgin Mary to inform her that the Messiah was to be born through her womb, he spoke to her in Davidic terms:

> "Don't be afraid, Mary," the angel told her, "for you have found favor with God! You will conceive and give birth to a son, and you will name him Jesus. He will be very great and will be called the Son of the Most High. The Lord God will give him the throne of his ancestor David. And he will reign over Israel forever; his Kingdom will never end!"

Gabriel's words constituted a clear announcement that Mary's child would come into this world to fulfill the promise given to David that one of his descendants would sit on his throne and rule over his kingdom. Mary, a devout young Jew who would have been aware of the Davidic covenant, must have deeply contemplated this stunning and wondrous revelation. She responded to Gabriel's words with humility.

When the millennial kingdom is finally instituted after the second coming, these long-anticipated prophetic promises will be fulfilled. Christ will reign from the throne of David. *What an awesome thing to ponder!*

The End of the Times of the Gentiles

Christ's coming will also mean the end of the times of the Gentiles. As a backdrop, Jesus prophesied that during the tribulation period, "Jerusalem will be trampled down by the Gentiles until the period of the Gentiles comes to an end" (Luke 21:24). The phrase, "the period of the Gentiles" refers to the time of Gentile domination over Jerusalem. This period began with the Babylonian captivity that started in 606 BC. Gentile domination was well entrenched by AD 70, when Titus and his Roman warriors overran Jerusalem and destroyed the Jewish temple. This domination will last into the seven-year tribulation period (Revelation 11:2), and will not end until Christ's second coming.

To clarify, in our own day, the Israelis control much of Jerusalem. But they do not control the Arab quarter or the area of the temple site. Hence, the period of the Gentiles has not yet ended.

Jerusalem will one day be restored under the rule of the divine Messiah, Jesus Christ. In dire threat at Armageddon, the people of Israel will finally recognize their Messiah and plead for Him to return (they will "mourn for him as for an only son"—Zechariah 12:10; Matthew 23:37-39; see also Isaiah 53:1-9), at which point their deliverance will surely come (see Romans 10:13-14). These regenerated Jews will enter into Christ's millennial kingdom (see Daniel 7:22,27; Zechariah 14:5; Matthew 19:28), and the times of the Gentiles will forever be over.

"I Am Coming Soon"

The book of Revelation begins with these words: "This is a revelation from Jesus Christ, which God gave him to show his servants the events that must *soon take place*...he blesses all who listen to its message and obey what it says, for *the time is near*" (Revelation 1:1-3). Later, toward the end of Revelation, Jesus affirmed "Look, I am coming soon! Blessed are those who obey the words of prophecy written in this book" (22:7).

Some Bible interpreters known as preterists argue that because the book of Revelation refers to "events that must soon take place" and speaks of Jesus as "coming soon," then the book must refer to events of the first century—more specifically, to the destruction of Jerusalem in AD 70, and not to the end times. Otherwise, they reason, "soon" would not make any sense.

In the original Greek text, however, the term "soon" often carries the meaning "swiftly," "speedily," or "at a rapid rate." An example is Luke 18:8, where this word is used to indicate that justice was to be rendered *speedily*. It appears likely that in Revelation 1:1-3, the term is intended to indicate that when the predicted events first start to occur, they will progress swiftly, or speedily, or in rapid succession. This is in keeping with the fact that the tribulation period of which Revelation speaks lasts only seven years (see Daniel 9:27).

It is noteworthy that many events detailed in the book of Revelation did not occur in AD 70. For example, in AD 70, "one-third of all the people on earth" were not killed, as predicted in Revelation 9:18. Nor has "everything in the sea died," as predicted in Revelation 16:3. In order to explain these and countless other prophecies in the book of Revelation, preterists must resort to an allegorical interpretation, since none of the events happened literally in AD 70. (See my book *The 8 Great Debates of Bible Prophecy* for a fuller rebuttal of preterism.)

What about Jesus's promise in Revelation 22:7, "Look, I am coming soon"? Some Bible expositors suggest that from the human perspective, Jesus's return may not have come soon, but from the divine perspective, it will. We have been in the last days since the incarnation of Christ (Hebrews 1:2; James 5:3). Moreover, James 5:9 affirms that "the Judge is standing at the door." Romans 13:12 exhorts us that "the night is almost gone; the day of salvation will soon be here." First Peter 4:7 warns, "The end of the world is coming soon." In view of such verses, Christ is coming "soon" from the divine perspective.

Other scholars suggest that perhaps Jesus meant He was coming soon from the perspective of the events described in the book of Revelation. In other words, from the vantage point of those living during the tribulation period itself, Christ was coming soon.

Still others say that the main idea in these words is that the coming of Christ is imminent. This being the case, we must all be ready, for we do not know precisely when He will return.

Regardless of one's position, some wonder why the second

coming hasn't occurred yet. Second Peter 3:9 affirms, "The Lord isn't really being slow about his promise, as some people think. No, he is being patient for your sake. He does not want anyone to be destroyed, but wants everyone to repent." God's delay is allowing people plenty of time to turn to Him. Of course, the time will come when the delay will end, after which there will be no further opportunity to turn to Christ.

Once the "soon" coming of Jesus occurs, judgment follows: "Look, I am coming soon, bringing my reward with me to repay all people according to their deeds. I am the Alpha and the Omega, the First and the Last, the Beginning and the End" (Revelation 22:12).

There are two key observations we can make about Christ's affirmation here:

1. Christ will judge people following the second coming. It is likely that, in context, Christ is here referring specifically to the judgment of the Gentile nations (Matthew 25:31-46) and the judgment of the Jews (Ezekiel 20:34-38), both of which occur immediately after the second coming. These judgments will determine who among both the Gentiles and the Jews will enter into His millennial kingdom, and who will be sent into eternal punishment.

2. Names of deity are ascribed to Christ—"I am the Alpha and the Omega, the First and the Last, the Beginning and the End." When used of God or Christ, the first and last letters of the Greek alphabet—Alpha and Omega—express eternality and omnipotence. Just as the Father is eternal and omnipotent (all-powerful), so Christ is eternal and omnipotent.

The phrase "the First and the Last" is used of God Almighty in the Old Testament. God Himself affirmed: "I am the First and the Last; there is no other God" (Isaiah 44:6). He also said, "I alone am God, the First and the Last" (Isaiah 48:12). Christ's use of this title for Himself was undoubtedly intended to communicate His equality with the Yahweh of the Old Testament. Christ wanted

His followers to be absolutely assured that He is the all-powerful Sovereign King who will be victorious.

The final passage in which Christ affirms His "soon" coming is Revelation 22:20: "He who is the faithful witness to all these things says, 'Yes, I am coming soon!'" This reminds us of Revelation 3:14, where Jesus identified Himself as "the faithful and true witness." Because He is faithful and true, we can trust all He says about His second coming.

Don't Be Ashamed

As I bring this chapter to a close, I want to point you to a rather sobering warning Jesus gave His followers in Luke 9:26: "If anyone is ashamed of me and my message, the Son of Man will be ashamed of that person when he returns in his glory and in the glory of the Father and the holy angels" (compare with 1 John 2:28). One Bible expositor suggests, "It is possible for believers to temporarily cower in fear around unbelieving peers and act 'ashamed' of Jesus, as Peter did in his denials of Christ. In such cases a believer may suffer loss of heavenly reward (1Co 3:10-15; 2Co 5:10), but not suffer eternal punishment."[2] Let us not forget that "true discipleship requires utter selfless commitment to Christ, repudiation of the world for Christ, and unflagging loyalty to Christ."[3]

These are important words for us, especially given that today it is politically incorrect—in some cases, *outright dangerous*—to take a public stand for Christ. My friend, stay strong. Stay bold.

8

The Judgment of the Nations and the Millennial Kingdom

At His first coming, Jesus was a humble carpenter who rode on a donkey into Jerusalem (Matthew 21:7-11). At His second coming, Jesus will come as a glorious King of kings and Lord of lords, and He will be on a majestic white horse (Revelation 19:11-16). His judgment of the nations will take place immediately following the second coming.

In His Olivet Discourse, Jesus spoke the following prophetic words to His followers about this judgment:

> When the Son of Man comes in his glory, and all the angels with him, then he will sit on his glorious throne. Before him will be gathered all the nations, and he will separate people one from another as a shepherd separates the sheep from the goats. And he will place the sheep on his right, but the goats on the left. Then the King will say to those on his right, "Come, you who are blessed by my Father, inherit the kingdom prepared for you from the foundation of the world. For I was hungry and you gave me food, I was thirsty and you gave me drink, I was a stranger and

you welcomed me, I was naked and you clothed me, I was sick and you visited me, I was in prison and you came to me." Then the righteous will answer him, saying, "Lord, when did we see you hungry and feed you, or thirsty and give you drink? And when did we see you a stranger and welcome you, or naked and clothe you? And when did we see you sick or in prison and visit you?" And the King will answer them, "Truly, I say to you, as you did it to one of the least of these my brothers, you did it to me."

Then he will say to those on his left, "Depart from me, you cursed, into the eternal fire prepared for the devil and his angels. For I was hungry and you gave me no food, I was thirsty and you gave me no drink, I was a stranger and you did not welcome me, naked and you did not clothe me, sick and in prison and you did not visit me." Then they also will answer, saying, "Lord, when did we see you hungry or thirsty or a stranger or naked or sick or in prison, and did not minister to you?" Then he will answer them, saying, "Truly, I say to you, as you did not do it to one of the least of these, you did not do it to me." And these will go away into eternal punishment, but the righteous into eternal life (Matthew 25:31-46 ESV).

During the tribulation period, the nations will be composed of the "sheep" and the "goats," representing the saved and the lost among the Gentiles. They will be intermingled and require separation by a special judgment. Let's consider some of the details of this prophesied judgment.

Distinct from the Great White Throne Judgment

Some Christians have concluded that this judgment must be another way of describing the great white throne judgment in Revelation 20:11-13. A comparison of the judgment in Matthew with the one in Revelation reveals that this view is incorrect.

Different Time: The judgment of the nations will occur immediately following the second coming of Christ to earth (Matthew 25:31). The great white throne judgment, by contrast, will occur after Christ's 1,000-year millennial kingdom (Revelation 20:11-12).

Different Scene: The judgment of the nations will take place on earth (Matthew 25:31). The great white throne judgment, by contrast, will occur at the great white throne, which is specifically described as being separated from the presence of the earth ("the earth and sky fled from his presence"—Revelation 20:11).

Different Subjects: At the judgment of the nations, three groups of people are mentioned—the sheep, the goats, and the brothers (Matthew 25:32,40). The great white throne judgment involves only one group of people—the unsaved dead of all time (Revelation 20:12).

Different Basis: The basis of judgment at the judgment of the nations hinges on how people treated Christ's "brothers" (Matthew 25:40). The basis of judgment at the great white throne judgment will be one's works throughout life. Those present will be judged "according to what they had done, as recorded in the books" (Revelation 20:12).

Different Result: The result of the judgment of the nations is twofold: the righteous (the sheep) will enter into Christ's 1,000-year millennial kingdom on earth; the unrighteous (the goats) will be cast into the lake of fire. The result of the great white throne judgment is that the wicked dead will be cast into the lake of fire. (The righteous are not even mentioned; indeed, the righteous are not even there.)

Different Bodies: No resurrection from the dead is mentioned in connection with the judgment of the nations. Only Gentiles who are alive on earth at the time of Christ's second coming will be judged. By contrast, the wicked dead from all ages will be resurrected to face Christ at the great white throne judgment (Revelation 20:13).

Such factors show that the judgment of the nations and the great white throne judgment are two different judgments, separated by 1,000 years. To conflate these into a single judgment amounts to violating the scriptural injunction about "rightly dividing the word of truth" (2 Timothy 2:15 NKJV).

Who Are the "Brothers"?

During the tribulation period, people will not be able to buy or sell if they don't receive the mark of the beast (Revelation 13:16-17). Christians will need to act sacrificially toward those who have not taken this mark—including the "brothers" of Christ.

In the judgment of the nations, we find that one's destiny—entering Christ's millennial kingdom or being cast into the lake of fire—hinges on how one treated Christ's "brothers." *But who are these brothers?*

A comparison of Matthew 25:31-46 with the details of the tribulation as recorded in Revelation 4–19 suggests that the term "brothers" refers to the 144,000 men mentioned in Revelation 7—Christ's Jewish brothers who will bear witness of Him during the seven-year tribulation. The backdrop is that God had originally chosen the Jews to be His witnesses, their appointed task being to share the good news of God with all other people around the world (see Isaiah 42:6; 43:10). The Jews were to be God's representatives to the Gentile peoples. But the Jews failed at this task, and did not recognize Jesus as their divine Messiah at His first coming.

During the future tribulation period, these 144,000 Jews—who will become believers in Jesus the divine Messiah sometime following the rapture—will finally fulfill this mandate from God. They will be His witnesses all around the world, and their work will yield a mighty harvest of souls (see Revelation 7:9-14).

These witnesses—God's faithful remnant—will be protectively "sealed" by God. Seals in Bible times were signs of ownership and protection. These Jewish believers will be "owned" by God, and by His sovereign authority He will protect them during their time of service in the tribulation period (Revelation 14:1,3-4; see also 13:16-18).

It is possible that these Jews become believers in a way similar to that of the apostle Paul, himself a Jew who had an encounter with the risen Christ on the road to Damascus (see Acts 9:1-9). Interestingly, in 1 Corinthians 15:8, Paul referred to himself in his conversion to Christ as one "born at the wrong time." Some Bible expositors, such as J. Dwight Pentecost, believe Paul may have been alluding to his 144,000 Jewish tribulation brethren, who would be spiritually "born" in a way similar to him—only Paul was spiritually born far before them.

These sealed servants of God will apparently be preachers. They will fulfill Matthew 24:14: "The Good News about the Kingdom will be preached throughout the whole world, so that all nations will hear it; and then the end will come."

There have been some Bible expositors and teachers who have held that the term "brothers" in Matthew's Gospel refers not specifically to Jewish believers, but to any genuine follower of God. They suggested that the reference in Revelation 7:4 to the 144,000 who "were sealed from all the tribes of Israel" is simply a metaphorical reference to the church. However, the fact that specific tribes are mentioned along with specific numbers for those tribes removes all possibility that this is a figure of speech. Nowhere else in the Bible does a reference to the 12 tribes of Israel mean anything but the 12 tribes of Israel. The truth is that many of today's finest Bible scholars agree that the 144,000 of Revelation 7 are the "brothers" of Matthew 24, and they are redeemed Jews.

Bible expositor Stanley Toussaint comments, "It seems best to say that 'brothers of Mine' is a designation of the godly remnant of Israel that will proclaim the gospel of the kingdom unto every nation of the world."[1]

Bible expositor Merrill F. Unger likewise says this of Christ's "brothers":

> During the tribulation period, God will sovereignly call and save 144,000 Jews...So glorious and wonderful will be the ministry of the 144,000 saved Jews and so faithful will be their powerful testimony, the King on His throne of glory will not be ashamed to call them "My brothers." More than that, He will consider Himself so intimately united to them that what was done or not done to them is the same as being actually done or not done to Himself...
>
> The fact that the Lord's brothers endured hunger, thirst, homelessness, nakedness, sickness, and imprisonment suggests their fidelity to their newfound Savior and Lord. They proved their willingness to suffer for Him amid the terrible persecutions and trials of the tribulation through which they passed. They proved their loyalty to their King. He attests His identity with them.[2]

J. Dwight Pentecost agrees with this assessment:

> That phrase [*my brothers*] may refer to...the 144,000 of Revelation 7, who will bear witness of Him during the Tribulation. Such ones will be under a death sentence by the beast [or antichrist]. They will refuse to carry the beast's mark, and so they will not be able to buy and sell. Consequently, they will have to depend on those to whom they minister for hospitality, food, and support. Only those who receive the message will jeopardize their lives by extending hospitality to the messengers. Therefore what is done for

them will be an evidence of their faith in Christ, that is, what is done for them will be done for Christ.[3]

The Bible Knowledge Commentary adds further clarification:

> The expression "these brothers" must refer to a third group that is neither sheep nor goats. The only possible group would be Jews, physical brothers of the Lord. In view of the distress in the Tribulation period, it is clear that any believing Jew will have a difficult time surviving (cf. 24:15-21). The forces of the world dictator [the antichrist] will be doing everything possible to exterminate all Jews (cf. Rev. 12:17). A Gentile going out of his way to assist a Jew in the Tribulation will mean that Gentile has become a believer in Jesus Christ during the Tribulation. By such a stand and action, a believing Gentile will put his life in jeopardy. His works will not save him; but his works will reveal that he is redeemed.[4]

These 144,000 Jewish evangelists apparently emerge on the scene in the early part of the tribulation period, sometime after the rapture. Evidently they will engage in their work of evangelism early in the tribulation because some of their hearers will believe and become the martyrs of Revelation 6:9-11 in the first half of the tribulation.

The Result of the Judgment

The result of the judgment of the nations is twofold: the righteous (sheep) will enter into Christ's 1,000-year millennial kingdom; the unrighteous (goats) will be cast into the lake of fire. The righteous show, by their assistance to the 144,000 Jews, that they are true believers in God. The unrighteous, by contrast, show by their uncaring attitude toward the 144,000 that they are not true believers in God. The rest of the unrighteous dead (unbelievers) will eventually be resurrected and face Christ at the great white throne judgment following the millennial kingdom (Revelation 20:11-15).

It is important for us to not forget that our holy and righteous God is also a God of judgment. All people will be held accountable for how they lived during their earthly years. *Earthly choices have eternal consequences.*

Jesus's Teaching on the Millennial Kingdom

Following the second coming of Christ, Jesus will personally set up His kingdom on earth. In theological circles, this is known as the millennial kingdom (Revelation 20:2-7; see also Psalm 2:6-9; Isaiah 65:18-23; Jeremiah 31:12-14,31-37; Ezekiel 34:25-29; 37:1-13; 40–48; Daniel 2:35; 7:13-14; Joel 2:21-27; Amos 9:13-14; Micah 4:1-7; Zephaniah 3:9-20).

In the chronology of the book of Revelation, the millennial kingdom follows the second coming of Jesus Christ. Revelation 19 and 20 are chronological, with the second coming described in chapter 19 and the millennial kingdom described in chapter 20. The second coming will lay a foundation for the establishment of the millennial kingdom. Prophecy expert John F. Walvoord explained that the second coming...

> includes the destruction of the armies gathered against God in the Holy Land (Revelation 19:17,21), the capture of the Beast and the False Prophet and their being cast into the lake of fire (v. 20), the binding of Satan (20:1-3), and the resurrection of the martyred dead of the tribulation to reign with Christ a thousand years (vv. 4-6). A literal interpretation of Revelation 20:4-6 requires that Christ reign on earth for a thousand years following his second coming.[5]

Related to this, Jesus's words to the sheep in the judgment of the nations are recorded for us in Matthew 25:34: "Then the King will say to those on his right, 'Come, you who are blessed by my

Father, inherit the Kingdom prepared for you from the creation of the world.'" This verse is a bit controversial, because some people think "Kingdom" in this verse refers to heaven. It is reasoned that just as the unrighteous (goats) go into the lake of fire, so the righteous (sheep) go to heaven. There are many who hold to this view.

I am convinced, however, that Jesus was referring to the millennial kingdom in this verse—the same 1,000-year millennial kingdom mentioned in Revelation 20. Why do I say this?

First and foremost, Matthew—himself a Jew—wrote the Gospel of Matthew between AD 50 and 60 to convince Jewish readers that Jesus is the promised Messiah. It contains about 130 Old Testament citations or allusions, more than any other Gospel (for example, 2:17-18; 4:13-15; 13:35; 21:4-5; 27:9-10). Because Matthew was a Jew and was writing to convince Jews that Jesus is the promised Messiah, it stands to reason that when speaking of the "kingdom," he would speak of it as the Jews understood it. After all, a specific kingdom was promised to the Jews in Old Testament Scripture (see Genesis 12:1-3; 15:18-21; 2 Samuel 7:12-13; 22:51).

It is with this in mind that theologian Charles C. Ryrie commented that "Matthew uses 'kingdom' primarily in relation to the Messianic, Davidic, millennial kingdom."[6] He clarifies that "in Matthew the eternal kingdom is referred to infrequently (cf. 6:33; 12:28; 13:38, 43; 19:24; 20; 21:31)."[7] (That is, Matthew generally does not use the term "kingdom" in reference to heaven and the afterlife, but rather, refers to a literal, earthly, 1,000-year kingdom, as promised to the Jews.) Theologian Lewis Sperry Chafer likewise wrote: "There is no reason why the word *kingdom* should be given any other meaning in this passage than has been assigned to it throughout the Gospel by Matthew. The kingdom is Israel's earthly, Messianic, millennial kingdom."[8]

It is a fact that the Jews to whom the book of Matthew was addressed were looking forward to the messianic kingdom, and not something else. They were eagerly awaiting the long-prophesied King who would appear and reign from the Davidic throne.[9] The ancient Jewish mind would not have understood the reference to the kingdom in Matthew 25:34 in any other way.

We must not forget that Matthew began his Gospel by pointing to the Abrahamic and Davidic covenants. He opened with these words: "This is a record of the ancestors of Jesus the Messiah, a descendant of David and of Abraham" (Matthew 1:1).

The backdrop to understanding this verse is that there were two kinds of covenants in biblical days: conditional and unconditional. A *conditional* covenant is a covenant with an "if" attached. This type of covenant demanded that the people meet certain obligations or conditions before God was obligated to fulfill that which was promised. If God's people failed to meet the conditions, God was not obligated in any way to fulfill the promise.

In contrast, an *unconditional* covenant depended on no such conditions for its fulfillment. There were no "ifs" attached. That which was promised was sovereignly given to the recipient of the covenant apart from any merit (or lack thereof) on the part of the recipient. *The covenants God made with Abraham and David were unconditional in nature.*

Matthew, in beginning his Gospel with the mention of these covenants, was calling attention to the fact that Jesus came to fulfill these unconditional covenants made with Israel's forefathers.[10] That being so, it seems clear that Christ came to institute the messianic kingdom promised in these covenants.[11] This messianic kingdom is the same as the 1,000-year millennial kingdom in Revelation 20.

A Problem for Posttribulationism

To review, Christ, in His judgment of the nations, will separate the sheep from the goats based upon how they treated Christ's "brothers" (Matthew 25:31-46). The sheep (believers) will be invited directly into Christ's 1,000-year millennial kingdom *in their mortal (unresurrected) bodies*. We know they will be unresurrected because they will get or remain married, bear children, grow old, and die during the millennial kingdom (see Isaiah 19:24-25; 65:17-25). Obviously, such things could not happen if they were already resurrected.

Here, then, is a significant problem for posttribulationism: If the rapture happens after the tribulation period, at which point all believers are resurrected, then what mortal (unresurrected) believers are left to enter into Christ's millennial kingdom? If all believers are raptured at the second coming, then there are no believers left to enter the millennium in their mortal bodies.

This is no problem for pretribulationism, which teaches that after the rapture, many will become believers during the tribulation period (see Revelation 7:9-17). It is these post-rapture believers who will enter into the millennial kingdom in their mortal bodies.

Tying It All Together

In summary, we have seen that...

- Christ will judge the nations following His second coming, separating the righteous from the unrighteous.

- Those present will be judged according to how they treated Christ's "brothers"—the 144,000 Jewish evangelists mentioned in Revelation 7 and 14.

- The righteous (those who treated Christ's brothers well, thereby giving evidence they are believers) will be invited to enter into Christ's 1,000-year millennial kingdom.

- The unrighteous (those who did not treat Christ's brothers well, thereby giving evidence they are unbelievers) will be cast into eternal punishment.

- The facts about the judgment of the nations are incompatible with posttribulationism, but fit quite well with pretribulationism.

In the next chapter, we will turn to Christ's prophetic teachings on the intermediate state (a disembodied state following death), as well as the resurrections and judgments of both the righteous and unrighteous.

9

The Intermediate State, Resurrections, and Judgments

The study of prophecy or the end times is known in theological circles as *eschatology*. This term is derived from two Greek words: *eschatos*, meaning "last" or "last things," and *logos*, meaning "study of." Eschatology is the study of last things.

Eschatology can logically be broken down into two primary fields of study. *General eschatology* concerns general matters such as the rapture, the tribulation, the second coming of Christ, the millennial kingdom, and the eternal state. In this book, we've already addressed a lot of Jesus's teachings on issues related to general eschatology. *Personal eschatology* concerns such things as death, the intermediate state, resurrection, and the judgment each person will face. In this chapter, we'll narrow our focus to Jesus's teachings on personal eschatology.

The Intermediate State

Many people have wrongly concluded that immediately following the moment of death, they will receive their resurrection bodies.

That is not the case, for the day of resurrection is yet future for all of us.

The state of our existence between physical death and the future resurrection is properly called the *intermediate state*. It is an *in-between* state—that is, it is the state of our existence in between the time our mortal bodies die and the time we receive our resurrection bodies in the future (see Revelation 6:9-11).

The intermediate state is a *disembodied* state. It is a state in which one's physical body is in the grave on earth while one's spirit or soul is either in heaven with Christ (2 Corinthians 5:8; Philippians 1:21-23) or in a place of great suffering apart from Christ (Luke 16:19-31; 2 Peter 2:9). One's destiny in the intermediate state depends wholly upon whether one has placed faith in Jesus Christ for salvation during one's earthly existence (Acts 16:31).

To clarify, human beings have both a material part and an immaterial part. A person's material part is his or her body. The immaterial part is the soul or spirit (these terms are used inter-changeably in Scripture). At the moment of death, a person's immaterial part—the soul or spirit—departs or separates from the material part, just as easily as a hand slips out of a glove (Genesis 35:18). (The Greek word translated "death" means "separa-tion.") At death, a human being becomes disembodied when his or her spirit or soul departs from the physical body.

There are many verses in Scripture that speak of the departure of the spirit from the body at death. The writer of Ecclesiastes—"the preacher"—tells us that at the moment of death, "the spirit will return to God who gave it" (Ecclesiastes 12:7). At the moment of His death, Jesus prayed, "Father, I entrust my spirit into your hands" (Luke 23:46). When Stephen was dying after being stoned, he prayed: "Lord Jesus, receive my spirit" (Acts 7:59).

This separation of the spirit from the physical body is only tem-porary. Scripture reveals there is a day coming in which God will reunite each person's soul or spirit to a resurrection body (John 5:28-29; 1 Thessalonians 4:13-17). When that day arrives, human beings will never again be in a situation where they are disembodied. They will live forever in their resurrection bodies.

This means that resurrected believers will live forever in the immediate presence of God (Revelation 21). Resurrected unbelievers will spend eternity in a place of great suffering, the lake of fire (20:15).

With this as our backdrop, let's now zero in on what Jesus had to say about the intermediate state. His most comprehensive teaching on the subject is found in Luke 16:19-31, in His parable of the rich man and Lazarus:

> Jesus said, "There was a certain rich man who was splendidly clothed in purple and fine linen and who lived each day in luxury. At his gate lay a poor man named Lazarus who was covered with sores. As Lazarus lay there longing for scraps from the rich man's table, the dogs would come and lick his open sores.
>
> "Finally, the poor man died and was carried by the angels to sit beside Abraham at the heavenly banquet. The rich man also died and was buried, and he went to the place of the dead. There, in torment, he saw Abraham in the far distance with Lazarus at his side.
>
> "The rich man shouted, 'Father Abraham, have some pity! Send Lazarus over here to dip the tip of his finger in water and cool my tongue. I am in anguish in these flames.'
>
> "But Abraham said to him, 'Son, remember that during your lifetime you had everything you wanted, and Lazarus had nothing. So now he is here being comforted, and you are in anguish. And besides, there is a great chasm separating us. No one can cross over to you from here, and no one can cross over to us from there.'

"Then the rich man said, 'Please, Father Abraham, at least send him to my father's home. For I have five brothers, and I want him to warn them so they don't end up in this place of torment.'

"But Abraham said, 'Moses and the prophets have warned them. Your brothers can read what they wrote.'

"The rich man replied, 'No, Father Abraham! But if someone is sent to them from the dead, then they will repent of their sins and turn to God.'

"But Abraham said, 'If they won't listen to Moses and the prophets, they won't be persuaded even if someone rises from the dead.'"

In this parable, the redeemed (Abraham and Lazarus) are portrayed as conscious and comfortable. There is no suffering for them. By contrast, we discern a number of sobering facts about unbelievers in the intermediate state:

- They consciously suffer in agony.
- They cannot be comforted.
- There is no possibility of them leaving the place of torment.
- There is no possibility of them contacting people on earth to warn them.
- The wicked dead are entirely responsible for not having listened to the warnings of Scripture in time—that is, while they were alive on earth.

Probably the worst torment the unbeliever will experience—both in the intermediate state and in the eternal state (the lake of fire) that follows—will be the perpetual knowledge that he or she could have trusted in Christ for salvation and thus escaped eternal punishment. *How tragic!*

Consciousness in the Intermediate State

Some Christians deny the idea of conscious suffering of the wicked in the intermediate state. They typically believe in what is called "soul sleep"—that is, the soul *goes to sleep* during the intermediate state, and hence is not conscious. The soul allegedly does not become conscious again until the future resurrection.

The parable of the rich man and Lazarus contradicts this idea. However, Christians who believe in soul sleep attempt to argue that because Jesus's words are part of a parable—*because Jesus is just telling a story*—He was not communicating literal truth about the intermediate state.

The problem with this viewpoint is that when Jesus taught through parables, He always cited real-life situations. For example, Jesus spoke of a prodigal son who returned home after squandering his money (Luke 15:11-32), a man who found a buried treasure in a field (Matthew 13:44), a king who put on a wedding feast for his son (Matthew 22:1-14), a slave owner who traveled abroad and then returned home to his slaves (Matthew 25:14-30), a man who constructed a vineyard (Matthew 20:1-16), and so on. All of these were common real-life occurrences in Bible days.

Jesus never illustrated His teachings with a fairy tale. This being the case, Luke 16 must be seen as a real-life situation and should be taken as solid evidence for conscious existence after death. Any other interpretation makes an absurdity of the text.

Besides, what Jesus taught about the rich man's suffering in Luke 16:19-31 is in perfect keeping with other clear verses on the subject. For example, the state of the ungodly dead in the intermediate state is described in 2 Peter 2:9: "The Lord knows how to…keep the unrighteous under punishment until the day of judgment" (ESV). The Greek word translated "keep" is in the present tense, indicating that unbelievers are held captive *continuously*. Peter is portraying them as condemned prisoners—fully conscious—being closely guarded in a spiritual jail while awaiting future sentencing and final judgment.

While God holds them there, their punishment continues. The present tense used in 2 Peter 2:29 points to the perpetual, ongoing nature of the punishment. While this punishment in the intermediate state is only temporary, we will see a bit later in the chapter that the wicked dead will eventually be resurrected and face Christ at the great white throne judgment, after which time their eternal punishment will begin in the lake of fire (Revelation 20:11-15).

In contrast to all of this, the intermediate state for Christians is supremely blissful. That's because they will be with Christ. Jesus told the thief on the cross (who had expressed faith in Him), "I assure you, today you will be with me in paradise" (Luke 23:43). While being stoned to death, Stephen prayed, "Lord Jesus, receive my spirit" (Acts 7:59). The apostle Paul said, "I long to go and be with Christ, which would be far better for me" (Philippians 1:23; see also Revelation 6:9-10). Paul also said, "We would rather be away from these earthly bodies, for then we will be at home with the Lord" (2 Corinthians 5:8). At the moment a Christian dies, then, his or her spirit slips out of the physical body and goes immediately into the presence of Christ in heaven. *Glorious!*

Having said all this, I must clarify that the term *sleep* is indeed used of death in the Bible, but we must correctly understand what is being communicated. Consider these representative verses:

- "Many of those who sleep in the dust of the earth shall awake, some to everlasting life, and some to shame and everlasting contempt" (Daniel 12:2 ESV).

- "Our friend Lazarus has fallen asleep, but I go to awaken him" (John 11:11 ESV).

- "Many bodies of the saints who had fallen asleep were raised" (Matthew 27:52 ESV).
- "As they were stoning Stephen, he called out, 'Lord Jesus, receive my spirit.' And falling to his knees he cried out with a loud voice, 'Lord, do not hold this sin against them.' And when he had said this, he fell asleep" (Acts 7:59-60 ESV).

Notice that while the Scriptures never speak of the soul sleeping (in unconsciousness), they *do* speak of the body sleeping. This is because the body takes on the appearance of sleep at the moment of death. These bodies will be "awakened" one day in the resurrection. This means that when you die, your physical body will take on the appearance of sleep while your spirit is either consciously with the Lord in heaven (if you're a Christian), or consciously in a place of suffering (if you're not a Christian).

This is illustrated for us with the Christian martyrs mentioned in Revelation 6:9-11:

> I saw under the altar the souls of all who had been martyred for the word of God and for being faithful in their testimony. They shouted to the Lord and said, "O Sovereign Lord, holy and true, how long before you judge the people who belong to this world and avenge our blood for what they have done to us?"

Though the physical bodies of these martyrs were killed, and hence took on the appearance of sleep on the earth, their souls or spirits were taken up to heaven, and are consciously able to speak to God.

The Resurrection of All People

Jesus taught that both Christians and unbelievers will one day be resurrected from the dead: "The time is coming when all the dead in their graves will hear the voice of God's Son, and they will rise again. Those who have done good will rise to experience eternal life, and those who have continued in evil will rise to experience judgment" (John 5:28-29).

The book of Revelation, which contains Christ's prophetic revelations given to the apostle John (Revelation 1:1-2), calls these resurrections the "first resurrection" and the "second resurrection" (Revelation 20:5-6,11-15). It is important to grasp that even though all Christians will be resurrected in the first resurrection, not all Christians will be resurrected at the same time. For example, there is one resurrection of believers at the rapture, before the tribulation period (1 Thessalonians 4:16; see also Job 19:25-27; Psalm 49:15; Daniel 12:2; Isaiah 26:19; John 6:39-40,44,54; 1 Corinthians 15:42). There is another resurrection of believers who lived and died during the tribulation period; they will be resurrected prior to the beginning of the millennial kingdom (Revelation 20:4). There is yet another resurrection at the end of the millennial kingdom (Revelation 20:4). These are all part of the first resurrection because they all occur before the second (final) resurrection of the wicked. For this reason, we can say that the term "first resurrection" applies to all the resurrections of the righteous, regardless of when they occur.

Though Jesus very clearly spoke of the reality of the Christian's resurrection body, He did not specifically address the nature of this body. He left that to His spokesman—the apostle Paul—who tells us a lot of what we need to know in 1 Corinthians 15:42-43. Using the analogy of a planted seed yielding a plant coming out of the soil, Paul said, "Our earthly bodies are planted in the ground when we die, but they will be raised to live forever. Our bodies are buried in brokenness, but they will be raised in glory. They are buried in weakness, but they will be raised in strength." What a forceful statement this is of the nature of our future resurrection bodies!

Paul noted that our present bodies will perish and die. The seeds of disease and death are ever upon them. It is a constant struggle to fight off dangerous infections. We often get sick. And eventually, all of us will die. It is just a question of time. Our new resurrection bodies, however, will be raised *imperishable*. They will be raised to live forever. All liability to disease and death will be forever gone. Never again will we have to worry about infections or passing away. Our new bodies will not be subject to aging, decay, or death. Never again will our bodies be buried in the ground.

Paul also noted that our present bodies are characterized by weakness. From the moment we are born, "our bodies are dying" (2 Corinthians 4:16; see also 1:8-9). Vitality decreases, illness comes, and old age follows, with its wrinkles and decrepitude. Eventually, in old age, we may become utterly incapacitated, not able to move around and do the simplest of tasks.

By contrast, our resurrection bodies will have great power. As Christian author J. Oswald Sanders put it, "Our new body, like our Lord's, will be characterized by power. Sleep will not be necessary to relieve weariness or recoup spent energy. Our abilities will be enlarged and we will throw off the limitations of which we are so conscious in life on earth."[1] Never again will we tire, become weak, or become incapacitated. Words truly seem inadequate to describe the incredible differences between our present bodies (those that will be "sown" in the earth) and our future resurrection bodies.

Best of all, our resurrection bodies will utterly defeat death. The apostle Paul put it this way: "When our dying bodies have been transformed into bodies that will never die, this Scripture will be fulfilled: 'Death is swallowed up in victory. O death, where is your victory? O death, where is your sting?'" (1 Corinthians 15:54-55). Theologian Wayne Grudem has some wonderful words related to this passage:

The fact that our new bodies will be "imperishable" means that they will not wear out or grow old or ever be subject to any kind of sickness or disease. They will be completely healthy and strong forever. Moreover, since the gradual process of aging is part of the process by which our bodies now are subject to "corruption," it is appropriate to think that our resurrection bodies will have no sign of aging, but will have the characteristics of youthful but mature manhood or womanhood forever.[2]

An interesting fact about the resurrection body is that there will be no further procreation among human beings. In Matthew 22:30, Jesus Himself affirmed, "When the dead rise, they will neither marry nor be given in marriage. In this respect they will be like the angels in heaven." The context here indicates that once believers receive their glorified resurrection bodies, the need for procreation—one of the fundamental purposes for marriage (Genesis 1:28)—will no longer exist. We will be "like" the angels in the sense that we will not be married and will not procreate any longer. (We know that angels do not procreate and reproduce, for all the angels in the universe were created at the same time—see Psalm 148:2-5; Colossians 1:16.)

Of course, it will always be true that my wife, Kerri, and I were married on this earth. Nothing will ever change that. And in the eternal state, in the new heavens and the new earth, we will apparently retain our memory that we were married on the old earth. It will be an eternal memory. And what a precious memory it will be.

We should not think of "no more marriage in heaven" as a deprivation. It may be very difficult for us to conceive how we could be happy and fulfilled if we were not still married to our present spouses. But God Himself has promised that not only will there not be any sense of deprivation, there will be only bliss, and there will be no more sorrow or pain.

My wife and I are part of the glorious church, which, according to the Scriptures, will one day be married to Christ. This event is referred to as the marriage of the Lamb (Revelation 19:7-9).

Now, in dire contrast to the first resurrection involving all believers, the second resurrection is a sobering thing to ponder. It is described in Revelation 20:13: "The sea gave up its dead, and death and the grave gave up their dead. And all were judged according to their deeds" (see also John 5:28-29). The unsaved of all time—regardless of what century they lived in, whether before the time of Christ or after—will be resurrected at the end of Christ's millennial kingdom. They will then face judgment at the great white throne judgment.

The Great White Throne Judgment

Unbelievers, following their resurrection, will face a horrific judgment that leads to their being cast into the lake of fire. This is called the great white throne judgment (Revelation 20:11-15). Christ, the divine Judge, will judge the unsaved dead of all time at the end of the millennial kingdom.

Those who face Christ at this judgment will be judged on the basis of their works (Revelation 20:12-13). It is critical to understand that their verdict is based on the fact they are *already unsaved*. This judgment will not separate believers from unbelievers, for all who experience it will have already made the choice, during their lifetimes, to reject God. Once they are before the divine Judge, they will be judged according to their works not only to justify their condemnation, but to determine the degree to which they should be punished throughout eternity (Matthew 10:15; 11:21-24; 16:27; Luke 12:47-48; John 15:22).

When Christ opens the Book of Life, no name of anyone present at the great white throne judgment is in it (Revelation 20:15). Their names do not appear in the Book of Life because they have rejected the source of life—Jesus Christ. As a result, they will be cast into the lake of fire—which constitutes the "second death" and involves eternal separation from God.

A sobering aspect of Christ's judgment of the wicked involves professed believers who are not true believers at all. Christ said, "On judgment day many will say to me, 'Lord! Lord! We prophesied in your name and cast out demons in your name and performed many miracles in your name.' But I will reply, 'I never knew you. Get away from me, you who break God's laws'" (Matthew 7:22).

In context, Jesus was dealing with the Pharisees, whom He categorized as false prophets (Matthew 7:15). While these individuals may have claimed to be God's representatives with God's message, in fact they were not at all what they appeared to be. They were ferocious wolves who had come to destroy God's flock (see Matthew 23:4-36). They were full of hypocrisy and unrighteousness. Despite all their external righteous claims, Christ—in Matthew 7:21-23—indicated that mere lip service is not enough.

The lesson we learn here is that many people may make an outward profession of faith and even give an external appearance of being devout without ever having entered into a real relationship with Jesus Christ. At the great white throne judgment, Jesus will say to them, "I never knew you."

All who participate in the great white throne judgment are "those who have continued in evil" and they "will rise to experience judgment" (John 5:29). I hate to even think about it. The wicked will be given resurrected bodies that will last forever, but bodies that are subject to pain and suffering, and they will spend eternity in the lake of fire. Their experience will involve weeping and gnashing of teeth (Matthew 13:41-42), condemnation (Matthew 12:36-37), destruction (Philippians 1:28), eternal punishment (Matthew 25:46), separation from God's presence (2 Thessalonians 1:8-9), and trouble and distress (Romans 2:9). *Woe unto the wicked.*

The Judgment Seat of Christ

All believers will one day stand before the judgment seat of Christ (also known as the *bema* seat) (Romans 14:8-10; 1 Corinthians 3:11-15; 9:24-27). At that time, each believer's life will be examined with regard to deeds done while in the body. Personal motives and intents of the heart will also be weighed.

The idea of a judgment seat relates to the athletic games of Paul's day. After the games concluded, a dignitary took his seat on an elevated throne in the arena. One by one the winning athletes came up to the throne to receive a reward—usually a wreath of leaves, a victor's crown. In the case of Christians, each of us will stand before Christ the Judge and receive (or lose) rewards.

While Jesus Himself does not tell us much about His judgment of Christians, we know with certainty that He is the Judge before whom we must appear. Jesus said, "The Father judges no one. Instead, he has given the Son absolute authority to judge" (John 5:22). "My Father has entrusted everything to me" (Matthew 11:27). "The Son of Man...will judge all people according to their deeds" (Matthew 16:27). "I have been given all authority in heaven and on earth" (Matthew 28:18). These truths were confirmed by the apostle Paul, who said that Christians "must all stand before Christ to be judged. We will each receive whatever we deserve for the good or evil we have done in this earthly body" (2 Corinthians 5:10).

The judgment seat of Christ has nothing to do with whether or not the Christian will remain saved. Those who have placed faith in Christ are saved, and nothing threatens that. Believers are eternally secure in their salvation (John 10:28-30; Romans 8:29-39; Ephesians 1:13; 4:30; Hebrews 7:25). This judgment rather has to do with the reception or loss of rewards.

The Eternal Rewards

Scripture often speaks of the rewards in terms of crowns that we wear. The *crown of life* will be given to those who persevere under trial, and especially to those who suffer to the point of death (James 1:12; Revelation 2:10). The *crown of glory* will be given to those who faithfully and sacrificially minister God's Word to the flock (1 Peter 5:4). The *crown incorruptible* will be given to those who win the race of temperance and self-control (1 Corinthians 9:25). The *crown of righteousness* will be given to those who long for the second coming of Christ (2 Timothy 4:8).

Be encouraged, dear Christian. Your God loves you and utterly delights in your spiritual successes, yearning to reward you one day. Let us therefore resolve to serve Him with joy and gladness, and with the full conviction that He always seeks our highest good— both here on earth and in our future in heaven. *Our God is an awesome God!*

10

The Eternal State

Scripture informs us that there is both an eternal state for the redeemed and an eternal state for the lost. The eternal state for the redeemed refers to Christians residing in heaven, where they will enjoy being face to face with Christ for all eternity. The eternal state for the lost refers to unbelievers residing in hell—the lake of fire—where they will suffer for all eternity.

This is a sobering topic. Jesus taught a great deal about both eternal states.

Heaven for the Redeemed

Who better to teach us about heaven than the very one who came from heaven? In John 3:13, Jesus affirmed, "No one has ever gone to heaven and returned. But the Son of Man has come down from heaven." Indeed, He is "the one who comes down from heaven and gives life to the world" (John 6:33). He said, "I have come down from heaven to do the will of God who sent me, not to do my own will" (John 6:38). He likewise said, "I am the living bread that came down from heaven" (John 6:51). He assured people that "I have come to you from God" (John 8:42), and "I came from the Father into the world" (John 16:28). Because Christ resided in heaven for all eternity past prior to His human birth on earth (in the incarnation), Jesus knows everything there is to know about heaven. He is our ideal teacher.

Heaven Is Paradise

Jesus was crucified between two criminals. One of them—before dying—believed in Jesus, and turned to Him and said, "Jesus, remember me when you come into your Kingdom" (Luke 23:42). Jesus replied to him, "I assure you, today you will be with me in paradise" (verse 43).

Here, the word "paradise" means "garden of pleasure" or "garden of delight." It is a term metaphorically used of heaven. In fact, Jesus Himself described heaven as the "paradise of God" (Revelation 2:7). It is a place of incredible bliss and serene rest in the very presence of God.

The apostle Paul said, "I was caught up to paradise and heard things so astounding that they cannot be expressed in words, things no human is allowed to tell" (2 Corinthians 12:4). Apparently this paradise of God is so resplendently glorious, so ineffable, so wondrous that Paul was forbidden by the Lord to say anything about it to those still in the earthly realm. Maybe this explains why Paul was so anxious to get back there. He affirmed, "I long to go and be with Christ, which would be far better for me" (Philippians 1:23). Maybe this is why Paul said, "No eye has seen, no ear has heard, and no mind has imagined what God has prepared for those who love him" (1 Corinthians 2:9). What Paul saw instilled in him an eternal perspective that enabled him to face all the trials that lay ahead of him (Romans 8:18; 2 Corinthians 4:17).

Paradise is the seat and dwelling place of the divine Majesty. It is where the glorified Christ dwells, and is the residence of the holy angels. At the moment of death, Christians instantly enter this blessed dwelling place. *Death is therefore nothing to fear* (1 Corinthians 15:55).

Jesus Himself Is Creating Our Eternal Dwelling Place

In John 14:1-3, Jesus informed His followers,

> Don't let your hearts be troubled. Trust in God, and trust also in me. There is more than enough room in my Father's home. If this were not so, would I have told you that I am going to prepare a place for you? When everything is ready, I will come and get you, so that you will always be with me where I am.

As I noted earlier, Jesus, in John 14:1-3, was speaking in terms His Jewish followers would have readily understood. Scripture portrays Christ as the bridegroom (John 3:29) and the church as His bride (Revelation 19:7). Hebrew weddings had three phases: (1) The parents of the bride and groom legally consummated the marriage betrothal. Following this, the groom went to prepare a place for them to live in his father's house. (2) At an undisclosed time, the bridegroom came to claim his bride. (3) A marriage supper, often lasting several days, was then celebrated. All three of these phases are seen in Christ's relationship to the church, the bride of Christ.

1. Believers who live during the church age become a part of the bride of Christ (the church) under the Father's sovereign and loving hand. Meanwhile, the Bridegroom, Jesus Christ, prepares a place for them to live in His Father's house.

2. At an undisclosed time, Jesus the Bridegroom will come to claim His bride at the rapture and take her to heaven, where He has prepared a place (John 14:1-3). The marriage ceremony will then take place in heaven prior to Christ's second coming (Revelation 19:6-16).

3. Sometime during the interim between Christ's second coming and the beginning of the millennial kingdom, the glorious marriage supper of the Lamb will take place (see Daniel 12:11; compare with Matthew 22:1-14; 25:1-13).

There are other notable parallels. In the same way that Jewish grooms typically paid a purchase price to establish the marriage covenant, so Jesus Christ paid a purchase price—His own blood—for the church (Acts 20:28; 1 Corinthians 6:19-20). In the same way that Jewish brides sought to live in a sanctified way while awaiting their groom, so the church is declared sanctified and set apart as it awaits Christ the Bridegroom (Ephesians 5:25-27; 1 Corinthians 1:2; 6:11; Hebrews 10:10; 13:12). In the same way that Jewish brides were unaware of the exact time their grooms would come for them, so the church is unaware of the exact time Jesus the Bridegroom will come to rapture His bride.

Here is what's intriguing to ponder: *What kind of place is Christ preparing in the Father's house for us?* It is here that the book of Revelation—containing prophetic revelations communicated by Christ to John (see Revelation 1:1-2)—gives us a fuller picture.

The place Christ is preparing for us is called the "New Jerusalem." Perhaps the most elaborate description of this heavenly city is in Revelation 21:1-4. In this awe-inspiring passage, we are told that that the New Jerusalem will come down out of heaven—where Jesus Himself has constructed it—and it will rest upon the new earth. Once it is upon the new earth, we are assured that "God's home is now among his people! He will live with them, and they will be his people. God himself will be with them" (verse 3).

I believe the New Jerusalem will be a literal city—a real place where real resurrected people and a holy God will dwell together. A city has dwelling places, means of transportation, order (government), bustling activity, various kinds of gatherings, and much more. There is no warrant for taking the descriptions of the New Jerusalem as merely symbolic. Every description we have of this city points to a real place of residence.

This makes sense in view of the fact that you and I will have eternal physical resurrection bodies (1 Corinthians 15:50-55). People with physical bodies must live in a physical place. And that physical place will be the New Jerusalem (John 14:1-3; Revelation 21:1-4).

In the midst of this glorious city are redeemed humans, celestial angels, and God Himself, who is identified as the Alpha and Omega, the beginning and the end. The Alpha and Omega declares, "Look, I am making everything new" (Revelation 21:5).

The city is made of materials that are resplendently glorious:

> The wall was made of jasper, and the city was pure gold, as clear as glass. The wall of the city was built on foundation stones inlaid with twelve precious stones...The twelve gates were made of pearls—each gate from a single pearl! And the main street was pure gold, as clear as glass...The city has no need of sun or moon, for the glory of God illuminates the city, and the Lamb is its light (Revelation 21:18-23).

The fact that God's glory will illuminate this city is an awesome thing to ponder. Also, the city will be constructed of transparent gold, with transparent streets, and precious jewels scattered throughout. Imagine what it will be like as the divine glory shines all through the city, reflecting and refracting the light everywhere!

The eternal city will be immense: "Its length and width and height" are "each 1,400 miles" (Revelation 21:16). The city will be large enough to accommodate the redeemed of all ages. Today's highest skyscrapers are dwarfed by comparison. The Empire State Building in New York City, for example, is 1,454 feet high. Because the New Jerusalem will reach so high, it is likely that the city will have countless levels or stories. With our powerful resurrection bodies, we will have no trouble traversing about inside this massive city.

The city will feature "a river with the water of life, clear as crystal, flowing from the throne of God and of the Lamb" (Revelation 22:1). Some have taken this river to be merely symbolic, while others have taken it to be a real river. Perhaps the best approach is to take it both literally *and* symbolically. Perhaps this is a real river that symbolizes the rich abundance of the spiritual life of the redeemed in the eternal city. Just as a real river provides an ongoing outflow of thirst-quenching water on a sunny day, perhaps this river with the water of life symbolizes the perpetual provision of spiritual satisfaction and blessing among the redeemed.

Revelation 22:2 then speaks of "a tree of life, bearing twelve crops of fruit, with a fresh crop each month. The leaves were used for medicine to heal the nations." The Greek word translated "healing" in this verse is *therapeia*, from which the English word *therapeutic* is derived. The word carries the basic meaning of "health-giving." In the present context, it means that the leaves on the tree of life are spiritually health-giving to the redeemed peoples of the world.

The Key Feature of Heaven: Face-to-Face Fellowship with Jesus

A key feature of our eternal life in heaven will be our perpetual fellowship with Jesus. In His high-priestly prayer to the Father, Jesus said, "Father, I want these whom you have given me to be with me where I am" (John 17:24)—that is, in heaven. Earlier, Jesus—speaking of the rapture—had said, "If I go and prepare a place for you, I will come again and will take you to myself, that where I am you may be also" (John 14:3).

Paul affirmed this same truth. Speaking of the appeal of heaven, Paul said that "we would rather be away from these earthly bodies, for then we will be at home with the Lord" (2 Corinthians 5:8). He also said, "I long to go and be with Christ, which would be far better for me" (Philippians 1:23). Paul said that once we are "caught up in the clouds to meet the Lord in the air...then we will be with the Lord forever" (1 Thessalonians 4:17).

As glorious as heaven is, the greatest appeal of our new home is that we will be with our Lord, face to face. And our fellowship with Him will never again be broken.

Building Up Treasure in Heaven

Because life on earth is short, and life in heaven is both long and resplendently glorious, doesn't it make good sense to build up our treasures there? In Matthew 6:19-21, Jesus urged,

> Don't store up treasures here on earth, where moths eat them and rust destroys them, and where thieves break in and steal. Store your treasures in heaven, where moths and rust cannot destroy, and thieves do not break in and steal. Wherever your treasure is, there the desires of your heart will also be (see also Matthew 19:21; Mark 10:21; Luke 12:33; 18:22).

Such words call us to examine our lives and priorities. They require an eternal perspective. With this eternal perspective in mind, Paul urged Christians, "Set your sights on the realities of heaven, where Christ sits in the place of honor at God's right hand. Think about the things of heaven, not the things of earth" (Colossians 3:1-2).

The original Greek text of this passage is intense: "*Diligently, actively, single-mindedly* set your sights on the realities of heaven." It is also in the present tense, carrying the idea that we are to "*perpetually keep on* setting our sights on the realities of heaven...Make it an ongoing process." I can tell you that putting this passage into practice can make all the difference in how you live your life on this temporal earth.

A Heavenly Destiny—Only Through Jesus

Contrary to popular thought, not everyone goes to heaven. Only those who trust in Christ for salvation do. Jesus Himself said, "I am the way, the truth, and the life. No one can come to the Father except through me" (John 14:6). A bold Peter likewise proclaimed, "There is salvation in no one else! God has given no other name under heaven by which we must be saved" (Acts 4:12). The apostle

Paul agreed, and affirmed, "There is one God and one Mediator who can reconcile God and humanity—the man Christ Jesus" (1 Timothy 2:5).

Some people get twisted all out of shape and claim it is arrogant and narrow-minded for Christians to claim Jesus is the only way. The truth is, Christians are much like postal carriers. They only deliver the mail. They did not write the letter. Jesus wrote the letter, and there is no arrogance involved in simply passing it on to others.

While saying Jesus is the only way may seem narrow-minded, there are many narrow things in life that are not bad, but are in fact entirely good. Sometimes there is only one operation that can save your life. Sometimes there is only one road out of the forest. When I take a flight to the Dallas-Fort Worth airport, I desire the pilot to land only at that airport, and on the correct runway. I want my wife Kerri to remain faithful to me (her "one and only") for the rest of her life. All these things are narrow, but they're also good.

So it is with the wonderful gift of salvation in Jesus Christ. The same gift is offered to all people, and they must choose to accept or reject it. The act of sharing the news about this gift with other people does not make one a narrow-minded, arrogant person, but rather a caring person. That's why I'll continue to talk about Jesus as the only way for the rest of my life. I want as many people as possible to avoid hell, and end up in heaven!

Hell for Unbelievers

Someone said that hell is as awful as heaven is wonderful. Today it has become fashionable to deny that hell even exists. However, Jesus—who, as God, is all-knowing—tells us more about the reality of hell than anyone else in the Bible. One cannot so easily dismiss that which was so often and so clearly taught by the Lord Jesus.

The Scriptures (and Jesus) use a variety of words to describe the horrors of hell, including the fiery lake of burning sulfur (Revelation

19:20; 20:14-15), eternal fire (Matthew 25:41), fiery furnace (Matthew 13:42), flaming fire and eternal destruction (2 Thessalonians 1:8-9), and eternal punishment (Matthew 25:46). The greatest pain suffered by those in hell is that they are forever excluded from the presence of God. If ecstatic joy is found in the presence of God (Psalm 16:11), then utter dismay is found in the eternal absence of His presence.

Hell was not part of God's original creation, which He called good (Genesis 1:10,12,18,21). Hell was created later to accommodate the banishment of Satan and his fallen angels who rebelled against God (see Isaiah 14:12-20; Ezekiel 28:11-15). As Jesus put it, the place called hell refers to "the eternal fire prepared for the devil and his demons" (Matthew 25:41). Human beings who reject Christ will join Satan and his fallen angels in this infernal place of suffering (Revelation 20:11-15).

Gehenna

One of the more important New Testament Greek words for hell is *Gehenna* (Matthew 10:28). This word has an interesting history. For several generations in ancient Israel, atrocities were committed in the Valley of the Son of Hinnom—atrocities that included human sacrifices, even the sacrifice of children (2 Kings 23:10; 2 Chronicles 28:3; 33:6; Jeremiah 32:35). These unfortunate victims were sacrificed to the false Moabite god Molech (Jeremiah 7:31-34).

Eventually the valley came to be used as a public dump into which all the filth in Jerusalem was poured. Not only garbage, but also the bodies of dead animals and the corpses of criminals were thrown on the heap, where they—like everything else in the dump—would perpetually burn. The valley was a place where the fires never stopped burning. And a hungry worm could always find a good meal there.

In Hebrew, this place was originally called *Ge-ben-hinnom* ("the

Valley of the Son of Hinnom"—see Joshua 15:8). This was eventually shortened to the name *Ge-Hinnom*. The Greek translation of this Hebrew phrase is *Gehenna*, and this term became an appropriate metaphor for the reality of hell. Jesus Himself used the word 11 times as a metaphorical way of describing the eternal, flaming place of suffering for unredeemed humanity.

Debates on the Nature of Hell

A great deal of debate has erupted among Christians as to the nature of the "fire" of hell. Many Bible scholars have always believed the fire of hell to be literal. There are others, however, who argue that the term refers primarily to the wrath of God. Below are some of the verses cited in support of this view:

- "The LORD your God is a devouring fire; he is a jealous God" (Deuteronomy 4:24).
- "Our God is a devouring fire" (Hebrews 12:29).
- "His rage blazes forth like fire" (Nahum 1:6).
- "Who will be able to stand and face him when he appears? For he will be like a blazing fire that refines metal" (Malachi 3:2).
- "My anger will burn like an unquenchable fire because of all your sins" (Jeremiah 4:4).

In view of what these verses say, it may well be that the fire of hell is both literal and metaphorical. Seen in this light, the literal fire in hell is an expression of the wrath of God.

Another debate centers on how there can be literal flames in hell (which emit light) when hell is also described as "outer darkness" (Matthew 8:12). It appears that the term "outer darkness" is a metaphor representing the spiritual darkness of hell. The unrepentant wicked will spend eternity in this gloomy yet flaming place. It is said to be "outer" in the sense that it is far, far away from God and all that is good and holy. In short, the fire of hell makes hell a place of destruction and torment. Yet it is like outer darkness because it is far from God and is a place of eternal gloom and spiritual darkness.

Weeping and Gnashing of Teeth

Because of the horrors of hell, there will be perpetual "weeping and gnashing of teeth" among its inhabitants (Matthew 13:42; Luke 13:28). "Weeping" carries the idea of wailing, not merely with tears, but with every outward expression of grief. The weeping will be caused by the environment, the company, the remorse and guilt, and the shame of being in hell.

People gnash their teeth when they are angry. Those in hell will be angry at the sin that brought them there, angry at what they've become, angry at Satan and his demons for their temptations to do evil in earthly life, and angry over the fact they rejected their ticket out of hell—salvation in Jesus Christ.

Degrees of Punishment

Not all people in hell suffer with the same intensity. The Scriptures reveal that there will be degrees of punishment in hell. These degrees of punishment will be based on respective degrees of sinfulness, as well as on a person's response to greater or lesser light (or knowledge) from God's Word.

Scripture provides significant support for this idea. In Luke 12:47-48, for example, Jesus said, "That servant who knew his master's will but did not get ready or act according to his will, will receive a severe beating. But the one who did not know, and did what deserved a beating, will receive a light beating" (ESV). Likewise, in Matthew 11:20-24, Jesus spoke of things being more tolerable for some than for others on the day of judgment. Moreover, in John 19:11, Jesus spoke of greater and lesser sins, and thus greater guilt (see also Matthew 10:15; 16:27; Revelation 20:12-13; 22:12).

The theological backdrop to degrees of punishment in hell is that God is perfectly just. His judgments are fair. So, for example, when Christians face Jesus at the judgment seat of Christ, some will receive rewards, while others will suffer loss of rewards. Christ is fair in recognizing that some Christians live faithfully on earth while others do not. His judgment of them will reflect this reality. The same is true about the great white throne judgment. Christ will be fair and recognize that some unbelievers are more wicked than others. Hitler, for example, will be judged much more severely than a non-Christian moralist. The extent of Jesus's judgments upon the unsaved will reflect their degree of wickedness.

We might summarize the respective judgments this way: Just as believers differ in how they respond to God's law and therefore will receive varying rewards in heaven, so do unbelievers differ in their response to God's law and therefore will receive varying punishments in hell. Just as there are degrees of reward in heaven, so there are degrees of punishment in hell. Our Lord is perfectly just in all things.

Each lost sinner will receive exactly what is due him, and no one will be able to argue with the Lord or question His decision. As Bible expositor Warren Wiersbe put it, "At the White Throne, there will be a Judge but no jury, a prosecution but no defense, a sentence but no appeal. No one will be able to defend himself or accuse God of unrighteousness."[1]

Even though there will be degrees of punishment in hell, all who participate in the great white throne judgment have a horrific destiny ahead—one filled with weeping and gnashing of teeth (Matthew 13:41-42), condemnation (Matthew 12:36-37), destruction (Philippians 1:28), eternal punishment (Matthew 25:46), separation from God's presence (2 Thessalonians 1:8-9), and tribulation and distress (Romans 2:9). *Woe to all who enter the lake of fire.*

God Desires All to Be Saved

Having said all this, I want to emphasize that God does not want to send anyone to hell. That's why He sent Jesus into the world—to pay the penalty for our sins by dying on the cross (John 3:16-17). Unfortunately, not all people are willing to admit that they sin and are in need of forgiveness. They don't accept the payment Christ made on their behalf by dying on the cross. God therefore allows them to experience the results of their choice (Luke 16:19-31). As C.S. Lewis said, in the end, there are two groups of people. One group says to God, "Thy will be done." These people recognize they are sinners, have placed their faith in Jesus for salvation, and will live forever with God in heaven. The other group is comprised of those to whom God says, sadly, "Thy will be done!" These people have rejected Jesus and thus will spend eternity apart from Him.

The Error of Annihilationism

Some people, in an attempt to avoid the severity of the idea of eternal suffering in hell, subscribe to a theory called *annihilationism*. The doctrine of annihilationism teaches that man was created immortal. But those who continue in sin and reject Christ are, by a positive act of God, deprived of the gift of immortality and are ultimately destroyed. After they die, consciousness is snuffed out.

Jesus Himself clearly refuted this view. In Matthew 25:46, Jesus declared, "They will go away into eternal punishment, but the righteous will go into eternal life." By no stretch of the imagination can the punishment spoken of in Matthew 25:46 be defined as a nonsuffering extinction of consciousness. Indeed, if actual suffering is lacking, then so is punishment. Punishment entails suffering. And suffering necessarily entails consciousness. Certainly one can exist and not be punished; but no one can be punished and not exist. Annihilation means the obliteration of existence and anything that pertains to existence, such as punishment. *Annihilation avoids punishment, rather than encountering it.*

The Greek word translated "eternal," used here to speak of the eternal life of the righteous in Matthew 25:46, is the same word used with regard to the conscious punishment of the wicked. The word comes from the Greek adjective *aionion*, meaning "everlasting," "without end." The wicked will be consciously punished for all eternity, and not be annihilated out of existence.

Notice that there are no degrees of annihilation. One is either annihilated or not. By contrast, Scripture teaches that there will be degrees of punishment (Matthew 10:15; 11:21-24; 16:27; Luke 12:47-48; John 15:22; Hebrews 10:29; Revelation 20:11-15; 22:12). The fact that people will suffer varying degrees of punishment in hell shows that annihilation or the extinction of consciousness is not taught in Matthew 25:46 or anywhere else in Scripture. These are incompatible concepts. Moreover, one cannot deny that for a person who is suffering excruciating pain, the extinction of his or her consciousness would actually be a blessing—not a punishment (see Luke 23:30-31; Revelation 9:6). Any honest seeker after truth must admit that one cannot define "eternal punishment" as an extinction of consciousness.

My friend, heaven is real, and hell is real. Jesus clearly taught both. That means you and I must believe both. Because hell is as awful as heaven is wonderful, let's take every opportunity we can to share the good news of the gospel with others.

11

Lessons Learned from the Seven Churches, Part 1

So far we've explored Jesus's prophecies on the rapture, the tribulation period, the second coming, the various judgments, the millennial kingdom, the intermediate state, and the eternal state. We've also looked at a variety of prophetic parables, including the well-known parable of the fig tree. We've gleaned many insights from Jesus's prophetic Olivet Discourse, a variety of other prophetic teachings from Jesus as recorded in the four Gospels, as well as the book of Revelation, mostly chapters 4 through 22.

Why, then, do the last two chapters of this book focus on Revelation chapters 2 and 3? The answer is simple. These two chapters contain some of the most important life lessons in all of prophetic Scripture. They are filled with life-changing, transformative truths. Addressing these truths is, in my thinking, the best possible way to close a book that deals with Jesus and the end times. Jesus wants us to incorporate these truths into the fabric of our lives.

That said, let's take a moment to get oriented. In Revelation 1:19, Jesus said to John, "Write therefore the things that you have seen, those that are and those that are to take place after this" (ESV).

This short verse constitutes a concise outline of the entire book of Revelation. The phrase "the things that you have seen" points to the things John had just seen and recorded in chapter 1—most of which relate to the glorified Jesus in heaven. The phrase "those that are" points to the present state of the seven churches in Asia Minor as documented in chapters 2 and 3. The phrase "those that are to take place after this" addresses events that are in the prophetic future, as recorded in chapters 4 through 22. Our attention in this chapter will be devoted entirely to the things that "are"—Jesus's words to the seven churches in Asia Minor. We will see that Christ's words are not only prophetic, but full of life lessons for Christians in every generation of church history.

Jesus's Words to the Seven Churches

To the Church in Ephesus

Jesus first addressed the church at Ephesus. He began this way: "Write this letter to the angel of the church in Ephesus. This is the message from the one who holds the seven stars in his right hand, the one who walks among the seven gold lampstands" (Revelation 2:1).

The "angel" of the church could refer to a specific angel assigned by God to protect the church in Ephesus. More likely, the term refers to the human pastor of the church. After all, the word *angel* means "messenger," and pastors are responsible for delivering God's messages to the church body.

It was strategically important that a church be set up in Ephesus. This was a thoroughly pagan city famous for its temple that honored the Roman goddess Diana. False religion thrived in this city. The apostle Paul, during his third missionary tour, spent about three years in Ephesus building up the church there (Acts 19). Upon his departure, young Timothy—Paul's associate in ministry—pastored at Ephesus for another year (1 Timothy 1:3,20). Eventually Paul was imprisoned in Rome. During that imprisonment, in about AD 61, he wrote his epistle (letter) to the Ephesians.

Notice how Jesus described Himself: He "holds the seven stars in his right hand" (Revelation 2:1). Many see this as meaning that Christ sovereignly holds the pastors of the seven churches in His hands, watching over them and their respective churches. Christ is also said to walk "among the seven golden lampstands," a reference to the churches themselves. That He "walks" among them means He is intimately acquainted with all that goes on in each of them. He observes what is right and what is wrong in each church. *He sees all.*

Jesus then affirmed what the church was doing right:

> I know all the things you do. I have seen your hard work and your patient endurance. I know you don't tolerate evil people. You have examined the claims of those who say they are apostles but are not. You have discovered they are liars. You have patiently suffered for me without quitting (Revelation 2:2-3).

A little historical backdrop puts things into perspective here. Decades before Revelation was written, Paul warned the elders of the Ephesian church that false teachers would arise and seek to lead them astray (Acts 20:28-31; see also 2 Corinthians 11:13). The discerning believers at Ephesus took this to heart and made great efforts to oppose the teachings of the false apostles.

By contrast, true apostles were chosen messengers of Christ, handpicked by the Lord or the Holy Spirit (Matthew 10:1-4; Acts 1:26). They were the special recipients of God's self-revelation (1 Corinthians 2:13). They recognized their special divine authority (1 Corinthians 7:10; 11:23) and were authenticated by miracles (Acts 2:43; 3:3-11; 5:12; 9:32-42; 20:6-12).

Christ commended the Ephesian believers for patiently enduring through all their challenges. By the time the book of Revelation was written, the church at Ephesus had patiently remained faithful to the Lord for some 40 years. They hadn't given up. They hadn't quit.

Despite their great efforts in standing for truth, however, Christ also had some words of correction for the church:

> I have this complaint against you. You don't love me or each other as you did at first! Look how far you have fallen! Turn back to me and do the works you did at first. If you don't repent, I will come and remove your lampstand from its place among the churches (Revelation 2:4-5).

Just 30 years earlier, the church at Ephesus had been commended for the love it had shown to others and to the Lord (Ephesians 1:15-16). But now their love had waned. They needed to reinvigorate their love for Christ and for others.

How painful it must have been for the Ephesian believers to hear these words: "Look how far you have fallen!" (Revelation 2:5). In the original Greek text, this carries the idea, "*Keep looking* at how far you have fallen," or "*keep on remembering* how far you have fallen." The Ephesians were to never forget from whence they had fallen.

Christ then commanded, "Turn back to me and do the works you did at first" (verse 5). The phrase "turn back" means "repent." To repent means to change one's thinking, with a subsequent change in behavior (see Acts 3:19; 9:35; 11:21; 14:15; 15:19; 26:18-21; 1 Thessalonians 1:9; 1 Peter 2:25). These believers in Ephesus were to "change their mind" and get back to loving the Lord as they should.

If they failed to repent, Christ said He would remove their lampstand from its place among the churches. This apparently means that Christ would remove the church from its place of service and usefulness.

My friend, the key lesson we learn from Jesus's words to the Ephesians is that doctrinal accuracy and moral purity are very important, but these things are not enough. Supreme love for God and others is also necessary. Christianity is more than just being doctrinally correct. It involves an ongoing love relationship with the Lord. We need to burn this truth into our minds.

As if to encourage the church right after His words of correction, Jesus exhorted them, saying, "This is in your favor: You hate the evil deeds of the Nicolaitans, just as I do" (Revelation 2:6). The Nicolaitans were open to license in Christian conduct—including "free love." They also ate food sacrificed to idols and engaged in various forms of idolatry. That the Christians at Ephesus hated such teachings was a commendable thing in Christ's eyes.

Christ closed His message to the Ephesian church this way: "Anyone with ears to hear must listen to the Spirit and understand what he is saying to the churches. To everyone who is victorious I will give fruit from the tree of life in the paradise of God" (Revelation 2:7).

In Bible times, the word *hear* often implied *obedience* to that which was heard. Hence, the Ephesians were called to obey that which was revealed by God's Spirit—elsewhere called the "Spirit of truth" (John 15:26; 16:13).

Jesus promised a blessing to Christians who were conquerors or overcomers (Revelation 2:7,11,17,26; 3:5,12,21). To be a conqueror or overcomer is essentially the same as being faithful and obedient. Christians who are unfaithful and disobedient will suffer a loss of rewards, but not a loss of salvation (Romans 14:10,13; 1 Corinthians 3:10-15; 2 Corinthians 5:10).

The conquerors, or the faithful, are promised the freedom to partake of the tree of life. We first saw this tree in the Garden of Eden. It is a tree that bestows continuing life (Genesis 2:9,17; 3:1-24). It will appear again in the future eternal city of heaven known as the New Jerusalem (Revelation 22:2) which is "in the paradise of God" (Revelation 2:7). The word "paradise" means "garden of pleasure" or "garden of delight." It is a term used of heaven in 2 Corinthians 12:4. The Ephesians were thus given a strong motivation for faithfulness and obedience to the Lord.

To the Church in Smyrna

Jesus spoke the following words to the church at Smyrna:

> Write this letter to the angel of the church in Smyrna. This is the message from the one who is the First and the Last, who was dead but is now alive: I know about your suffering and your poverty—but you are rich! I know the blasphemy of those opposing you. They say they are Jews, but they are not, because their synagogue belongs to Satan (Revelation 2:8-9).

As noted earlier, the "angel" of the church could refer to a specific angel assigned by God to protect the church in Smyrna. More likely, however, the term refers to the human pastor of the church.

Smyrna was an important city in New Testament times. It was located about 35 miles north of Ephesus and was a prosperous commercial center. In this city, the imperial cult of ancient Rome brought severe persecution upon Christians who refused to say, "Caesar is Lord."

Jesus described Himself as "the First and the Last" (Revelation 2:8). He thereby indicated He is eternal God, who has always existed in the past and who will always exist in the future. God described Himself this way in the Old Testament—for example, "I am the First and the Last; there is no other God. Who is like me?" (Isaiah 44:6), and "I alone am God, the First and the Last" (Isaiah 48:12).

In a similar vein, Jesus referred to Himself as the one "who was dead but is now alive" (Revelation 2:8). He had been crucified (John 19:18,20,23,32,41), but was now risen from the dead (Matthew 28:9-10,16-20; Luke 24:13-43; John 20:11-17,26-29; 21:1-23; 1 Corinthians 15:5-6).

Christ informed the Christians at Smyrna, "I know about your suffering and your poverty" (Revelation 2:9). Because He possesses omniscient vision (Revelation 1:14), He is aware of all the circumstances of all believers (see Matthew 11:27; Luke 5:4-6; John 2:25; 16:30; 21:17; Acts 1:24). He was thus fully aware of all the sufferings of the Christians in Smyrna.

Christ informed these people that despite their suffering and poverty, they were "rich" (Revelation 2:9). Like all faithful believers, they had a large storehouse of eternal riches awaiting them in heaven (see Christ's words in Matthew 6:19-20).

Jesus made reference to those in Smyrna who "say they are Jews, but they are not, because their synagogue belongs to Satan" (Revelation 2:9). This apparently was a reference to apostate Jews. These Jews hated Christ and all who followed Him. They therefore slandered the Christians in Smyrna. These individuals were Jewish by physical lineage, but they did not hold to the religion of their Jewish ancestors, such as Abraham. They had become secularized by a pagan culture. Because they were engaged in false religion, they were instruments of the devil, and the synagogue they attended was in reality a habitat of the devil.

Jesus then exhorted the Christians in Smyrna,

> Don't be afraid of what you are about to suffer. The devil will throw some of you into prison to test you. You will suffer for ten days. But if you remain faithful even when facing death, I will give you the crown of life (Revelation 2:10).

The original Greek text of the phrase translated "don't be afraid" is more literally "*stop* being afraid." The believers in Smyrna were already experiencing fear. God knows in advance the sufferings His people will encounter (see Genesis 15:13; Acts 9:14). Christ knew in advance the suffering about to be experienced by the Christians in Smyrna. He thus exhorted them to not be afraid.

Their suffering was ultimately rooted in the work of the devil, a fallen angel who is aligned against God and His purposes. The word *devil* carries the idea of "adversary" (1 Peter 5:8). It may be that the devil motivated the apostate Jews to imprison the Christians in Smyrna (compare with Revelation 12:4,12; John 8:44; Acts 16:16-18).

The Christians in Smyrna were informed they would "suffer for ten days" (Revelation 2:10). This may refer to ten literal days of particularly intense persecution yet to come. Or it may refer to ten short outbreaks of persecution under ten Roman emperors: Nero, Domitian, Trajan, Hadrian, Septimus Severus, Maximin, Decius, Valerian, Aurelian, and Diocletian.

Christ thus exhorted His people, "If you remain faithful even when facing death, I will give you the crown of life" (Revelation 2:10). We are reminded that in the second century AD, the pastor of the church in Smyrna—Polycarp, a pupil of the apostle John—was burned alive for refusing to worship Caesar.

Those in Smyrna who remained faithful to Christ even in the face of death were promised the "crown of life" (Revelation 2:10). All believers will one day face the judgment seat of Christ (Romans 14:8-10; 1 Corinthians 3:1-10; 2 Corinthians 5:10). They will either receive rewards or forfeit them. One such reward is the "crown of life"—given to those who persevere under trial, especially to the point of death (James 1:12; Revelation 2:10).

Christ closed His message to the Christians in Smyrna this way: "Anyone with ears to hear must listen to the Spirit and understand what he is saying to the churches. Whoever is victorious will not be harmed by the second death" (Revelation 2:11).

Again, in Bible times, the word *hear* implied obedience. The Christians in Smyrna were called to obey that which was revealed to them by God's Spirit (2 Timothy 3:15-17; 2 Peter 1:21).

Christ affirmed that "whoever is victorious"—that is, those who are faithful and obedient—"will not be harmed by the second death" (Revelation 2:11). The first death is physical death—that is, the separation of the spirit or soul from the body (Genesis 35:18). Virtually all people (except Christians who take part in the rapture) will experience the first death (1 Corinthians 15:50-55; 1 Thessalonians 4:13-17). The second death—for unbelievers only—refers to eternal separation from God in the lake of fire, which is eternal hell.

The statement "Whoever is victorious will not be harmed by the second death" is a figure of speech in which a positive idea is emphasized by negating its opposite. We might illustrate this with the statement "I am not amused," which actually means, "I am annoyed." The Lord's point is that faithful believers may positively look forward to eternal life in heaven.

An important lesson we learn from Jesus's instructions to the Christians in Smyrna is this: *Don't sweat over earthly troubles. Our destiny in heaven is secure. Rejoice!* This is another truth we must burn into our minds.

I am reminded of Christ's words in the Gospels: "If any of you wants to be my follower, you must give up your own way, take up your cross, and follow me. If you try to hang on to your life, you will lose it. But if you give up your life for my sake, you will save it" (Matthew 16:24-25). It can be costly to live as a committed Christian. This is especially true as we draw nearer to the end times, for the persecution of Christians will increase. No matter what the world throws at us, however, our destiny is secure—and a glorious inheritance awaits us in heaven (Romans 8:18; 1 Peter 1:4). Never hesitate to take up your cross and follow Jesus on a daily basis (Matthew 16:24).

To the Church in Pergamum

Jesus next addressed the church at Pergamum: "Write this letter to the angel of the church in Pergamum. This is the message from the one with the sharp two-edged sword" (Revelation 2:12).

The angel of the church likely refers to the pastor of the church. Christ's identification of Himself as "the one with the sharp two-edged sword" alludes back to Revelation 1:16, where we read that "a sharp two-edged sword came from his mouth." Based on how the phrase is used in Revelation, it apparently means that Christ speaks forth words of judgment accompanied by disciplinary action.

Pergamum was an important city in New Testament times. It was located in northwest Asia Minor, and featured large buildings—including a library with more than 200,000 items. At one time, Pergamum was the capital city of the Roman province of Asia.

Christ said to the believers in this city, "I know that you live in the city where Satan has his throne, yet you have remained loyal to me. You refused to deny me even when Antipas, my faithful witness, was martyred among you there in Satan's city" (Revelation 2:13). It is noteworthy that Satan is not omnipresent like God is. He can be in only one place at a time. Perhaps at the time Christ spoke these words, Satan was localized in Pergamum.

This is certainly in keeping with the fact that Pergamum was the official center of emperor worship in Asia. The city also featured a temple that honored Asclepius, a pagan god whose symbol was that of a serpent (like Satan—see Genesis 3:1; 2 Corinthians 11:3). There was also a giant altar of Zeus that overlooked the city. With this abundance of false religion, it is not surprising that Satan had a throne there.

Satan is elsewhere called the "ruler of this world" (John 12:31) and "the god of this world" (2 Corinthians 4:4). He deceives the whole world (Revelation 12:9; 20:3). He has power in the governmental realm (Matthew 4:8-9; 2 Corinthians 4:4), the physical realm (Luke 13:11,16; Acts 10:38), the angelic realm (Ephesians 6:11-12; Jude 9), and the ecclesiastical (church) realm (Revelation 2:9; 3:9). His influence is immense.

Despite the rampant satanic and pagan influences in Pergamum, the believers who resided there remained loyal to Christ. They stood loyal even when Antipas—a Christian leader—was martyred by slow roasting inside a brass bull positioned over burning flames.

Despite their loyalty, Christ had words of correction for the church:

> I have a few complaints against you. You tolerate some among you whose teaching is like that of Balaam, who showed Balak how to trip up the people of Israel. He taught them to sin by eating food offered to idols and by committing sexual sin. In a similar way, you have some Nicolaitans among you who follow the same teaching (Revelation 2:14-15).

In Old Testament times, Balaam had been hired by Balak, the king of Moab, to lure the hearts of the Israelites away from the Lord God by having Moabite women seduce Israelite men into intermarriage (Numbers 22–25; 31). The Israelites succumbed to fornication and idolatrous feasts. The Nicolaitans were open to license in Christian conduct (including free love), ate food sacrificed to idols, and engaged in idolatry. Their influence had penetrated the church at Pergamum, and Christ would not have this.

Christ therefore urged, "Repent of your sin, or I will come to you suddenly and fight against them with the sword of my mouth" (Revelation 2:16). Repentance involves a change in one's thinking that is evidenced by changed behavior. Members of the church were called to repent of their openness to false teachings, which had led to inappropriate behavior. If they failed to repent, Christ would come in disciplinary judgment.

Here's an important truth we all need to remember: A failure to repent of sin always brings God's discipline in the life of a believer (see Psalm 32:3-5; 51; Hebrews 12:5-11). It therefore makes good sense to maintain a lifestyle of repentance before God. First

Corinthians 11:31 says, "If we would examine ourselves, we would not be judged by God in this way."

The believers in Pergamum were called to obey that which was revealed by God's Spirit (2 Timothy 3:15-17; 2 Peter 1:21). Christ promised, "To everyone who is victorious I will give some of the manna that has been hidden away in heaven. And I will give to each one a white stone, and on the stone will be engraved a new name that no one understands except the one who receives it" (Revelation 2:17).

This apparently means that Christians who are faithful and obedient will be rewarded at the judgment seat of Christ. The terminology used to describe this reward is interesting. Just as manna served as food sustained the Hebrews during the wilderness sojourn (Exodus 16:32-36; Hebrews 9:4), so Christ Himself—as spiritual bread—sustains believers today (see John 6:33,35,48,51). Believers in Pergamum who refused to participate in eating food sacrificed to idols would enjoy a much better banquet in heaven—featuring the hidden manna, Jesus Christ Himself.

The reference to the white stone could mean one of three things:

1. Victorious athletes in Bible times were given white stones that served as admission passes to a winner's celebration. The faithful believer's "white stone" may point to being admitted into the ultimate winner's celebration: *eternal life in heaven*.

2. In Roman arenas, gladiators who became favorites among the people were granted retirement from life-endangering combat. A white stone was given to them to symbolize this retirement. Perhaps believers who are engaged in battle against sin and an ungodly world will be granted "retirement" to heaven, where they will enjoy eternal rest (see Revelation 14:13).

3. In Bible times, judges would indicate the innocence of a person by placing a white stone in a vessel. Perhaps the white stone

represents the believer's assurance of being acquitted before God (see Romans 8:1).

To the Church in Thyatira

Next, Jesus shifted His attention to the church at Thyatira: "Write this letter to the angel of the church in Thyatira. This is the message from the Son of God, whose eyes are like flames of fire, whose feet are like polished bronze" (Revelation 2:18). The angel is likely the pastor of the church at Thyatira, which was located about halfway between Pergamum and Sardis. This city had been under Roman rule for centuries and was a thriving commercial center. Its primary industries were wool and dye (see Acts 16:14).

Jesus described Himself as the Son of God, which is a title of deity. Scripture elsewhere indicates that whenever Jesus claimed to be the Son of God, His Jewish contemporaries fully understood that He was making a claim to be God in an unqualified sense (see John 19:7; see also 5:18).

Jesus also said He has eyes "like flames of fire" (Revelation 2:18). This portrays Christ as having penetrating scrutiny in seeing all things as they truly are—something He will demonstrate at the future judgment (see 1 Corinthians 3:13).

Jesus, the all-seeing One, affirmed to the church at Thyatira, "I know all the things you do. I have seen your love, your faith, your service, and your patient endurance. And I can see your constant improvement in all these things" (Revelation 2:19). The church was clearly doing a lot of things right.

But Jesus also offered words of correction: "I have this complaint against you. You are permitting that woman—that Jezebel who calls herself a prophet—to lead my servants astray. She teaches them to commit sexual sin and to eat food offered to idols" (Revelation 2:20).

We recall from the Old Testament the idolatrous queen who

enticed Israel to engage in Baal worship (1 Kings 16–19). The evil woman of Revelation 2:20 may have been named Jezebel, or perhaps "Jezebel" was a pseudonym or nickname for this false prophetess—a *Jezebel-like* woman. She apparently promoted the idea that people could engage in sins of the outer body (such as sexual immorality) without doing injury to a person's inner spirit (see Acts 15:19-29).

An important lesson Christians can derive from this is that they should make every effort to abstain from fornication (Acts 15:20). In fact, they should *flee* it (1 Corinthians 6:13,18). Fornication should not even be named or spoken of among Christians (Ephesians 5:3).

Jesus then said of Jezebel, "I gave her time to repent, but she does not want to turn away from her immorality" (Revelation 2:21). God always provides people with ample time to repent (Genesis 15:16; Isaiah 48:9; Romans 2:4-5). Recall that He gave the Ninevites 40 days to repent, which they did, thus averting judgment (Jonah 3:4; see also Jeremiah 18:7-10). Unlike the Ninevites, Jezebel refused to repent, just like many others who have hardened their hearts against God (see 2 Kings 17:14; 2 Chronicles 28:22; 33:23; Nehemiah 9:29; Jeremiah 6:15; Daniel 9:13; Luke 16:31; Revelation 9:21).

God, of course, doesn't want people to perish. He typically delays judgment to give people time to repent. Second Peter 3:9 declares, "The Lord isn't really being slow about his promise, as some people think. No, he is being patient for your sake. He does not want anyone to be destroyed, but wants everyone to repent."

Because Jezebel refused to repent, Jesus had no alternative but to speak words of judgment and discipline:

> I will throw her on a bed of suffering, and those who commit adultery with her will suffer greatly unless they repent and turn away from her evil deeds. I will strike her children dead. Then all the churches will know that I am the one

who searches out the thoughts and intentions of every person. And I will give to each of you whatever you deserve (Revelation 2:22-23).

Let's not miss the irony of what is going on here. Jezebel promoted sexual immorality, a sin committed upon a bed. In judgment, she was to be thrown upon a sickbed. Jesus promised great distress.

When Jesus said, "I will strike her children dead" (Revelation 2:23), He was not referring to her physical offspring, but to her followers—all those who participate in her evil deeds.

Jesus then affirmed that nothing escapes God's (Christ's) notice. He has perfect knowledge of what transpires in every human heart (see Psalm 7:9; Proverbs 24:12). He promises a judgment that is just—commensurate with one's deeds (Matthew 16:27; Romans 2:6; Revelation 20:12).

Jesus knew that not all in Thyatira had been unfaithful to Him. He therefore provided a special word for them: "I also have a message for the rest of you in Thyatira who have not followed this false teaching…I will ask nothing more of you except that you hold tightly to what you have until I come" (Revelation 2:24-25). Christ did not wish to make their already-difficult lives even more so. He simply urged them to not give up in resisting evil.

Jesus then promised,

> To all who are victorious, who obey me to the very end, to them I will give authority over all the nations. They will rule the nations with an iron rod and smash them like clay pots. They will have the same authority I received from my Father, and I will also give them the morning star!

Faithful believers will reign with Christ in His future millennial kingdom (Revelation 20:6; see also 1 Corinthians 6:2-3; 2 Timothy

2:12; Revelation 3:21). Believers who do not remain faithful apparently forfeit participation in this reign.

Christ will also give faithful and obedient believers the "morning star." Christ Himself is the morning star (see Revelation 22:16). Though this morning star has already dawned in the hearts of believers (2 Peter 1:19), they will one day encounter the "star" directly and in fullness.

As noted earlier, the word *hear* often implied obedience. Hence, the Christians in Thyatira were called to obey that which was revealed by God's Spirit (2 Timothy 3:15-17; 2 Peter 1:21).

. . . .

In this chapter, we have seen the following:

- Christ, as all-knowing God, is aware of all that goes on in the churches.
- Christ commends churches whenever He can.
- Christ corrects churches when it is necessary.
- Christ offers people in the churches time to repent, but if repentance is not forthcoming, He brings discipline.
- Christ typically offers powerful incentives for faithfulness and obedience.

In the next chapter, we will consider three more churches—those in Sardis, Philadelphia, and Laodicea.

12

Lessons Learned from the Seven Churches, Part 2

In the previous chapter we considered Christ's words of commendation and correction to the churches at Ephesus, Smyrna, Pergamum, and Thyatira. We now continue with a consideration of His words to the churches at Sardis, Philadelphia, and Laodicea.

To the Church in Sardis

After addressing the church at Thyatira, Jesus turned His attention to the church at Sardis. Sardis was about 30 miles southeast of Thyatira. It was located at the foot of Mount Tmolus, on the river Pactolus. The primary business in this industrial city was harvesting wool, dying it, and making garments from it. From a religious standpoint, this city was heavily permeated by pagan worship.

Jesus described Himself as "the one who has the sevenfold Spirit of God and the seven stars" (Revelation 3:1). The seven spirits are apparently a metaphorical reference to the Holy Spirit in His fullness—seven being a number of completeness. Perhaps the Holy Spirit is mentioned because this church was utterly lifeless, and it is the Holy Spirit who can bring new life to believers (see Galatians

5:22-23). The seven stars are "the angels of the seven churches" (Revelation 1:20)—apparently the pastors of the seven churches.

Jesus told the church, "I know all the things you do" (Revelation 3:1). We recall that Jesus was previously described as having eyes "like flames of fire" (1:14)—that is, His penetrating gaze that enables Him to see all things as they truly are. He accurately diagnoses both the strengths and weaknesses of the seven churches.

The church members at Sardis must have dreaded hearing what Christ then said to them: "You have a reputation for being alive— but you are dead" (Revelation 3:1). There was no spiritual vitality in this church, even though there were a few genuine believers left (see verse 4). The church members were similar to the Pharisees: By outward appearances they seemed spiritual, but in reality they were spiritually dead (Matthew 23:27-28). They were hypocrites.

A hypocrite pretends to have virtuous character, when in reality that's not the case (see Revelation 3:1). Jesus spoke sternly against the religious hypocrisy of His day (Matthew 23:28; Mark 12:15; Luke 12:1). My friend, you and I should seek to avoid hypocrisy like the plague!

Understandably, Jesus urged the church members at Sardis,

> Wake up! Strengthen what little remains, for even what is left is almost dead. I find that your actions do not meet the requirements of my God. Go back to what you heard and believed at first; hold to it firmly. Repent and turn to me again (Revelation 3:2-3).

The works of these believers fell far short of what God required of them. They needed to awaken from their spiritual slumber and fan into a flame their dying embers of spiritual commitment (see Romans 13:11). They were urged to keep in mind their rich spiritual heritage and return to the attitudes and activities their teachers had taught them.

Repentance was the need of the hour—a change in thinking with a subsequent change in behavior. Immediate repentance was required by Christ, who warned, "If you don't wake up, I will come to you suddenly, as unexpected as a thief" (Revelation 3:3). In other words, if the church members failed to rectify things, Christ would bring swift judgment at a time when they would least expect it.

Thankfully, not all the church members were in this pathetic condition: "Yet there are some in the church in Sardis who have not soiled their clothes with evil. They will walk with me in white, for they are worthy" (Revelation 3:4). In Bible times, garments often metaphorically referred to a person's character. Soiled garments indicated a polluted character. This verse tells us that there were some in the church who had remained spiritually unstained (see Jude 23). They will be dressed in white (Revelation 6:11; 7:9,13; 19:8,14), which represents their imputed righteousness and purity.

Christ then made this promise to the faithful and obedient: "All who are victorious will be clothed in white. I will never erase their names from the Book of Life, but I will announce before my Father and his angels that they are mine" (Revelation 3:5). The promise about being "clothed in white" would have been especially meaningful to people who lived in a city where woolen garments were manufactured.

The clothing-character metaphor occurs elsewhere in Scripture. First Peter 5:5 exhorts, "All of you, dress yourselves in humility as you relate to one another." Colossians 3:12 says, "You must clothe yourselves with tenderhearted mercy, kindness, humility, gentleness, and patience" (see also Romans 13:14).

The faithful and obedient will never have their names blotted out of the Book of Life. This is a heavenly book in which are recorded the names of the redeemed who will inherit heaven (Revelation 3:5; 13:8; 17:8; 20:12,15; 21:27; see also Luke 10:20; Philippians 4:3). Christ's words include a Hebrew literary device in which a positive truth is taught by negating its opposite. The main idea is this: *Your names will always stay in the Book of Life.*

Christ also promised He would confess the names of the faithful and obedient before His Father and the angels (Revelation 3:5). We recall that in the Gospels, Christ similarly promised, "Everyone who acknowledges me publicly here on earth, I will also acknowledge before my Father in heaven" (Matthew 10:32).

As with the previous churches, Christ closed with these words to the church at Sardis: "Anyone with ears to hear must listen to the Spirit and understand what he is saying to the churches" (Revelation 3:6). Believers are called to hear and obey these prophetic revelations inspired by the Holy Spirit (2 Timothy 3:15-17; 2 Peter 1:21).

To the Church in Philadelphia

Next, Jesus shifted His attention to the pastor ("angel") of the church at Philadelphia, a city in Lydia, located in western Asia Minor, about 28 miles from Sardis. Its major industry was wine, and its chief pagan deity was the god of wine, Dionysus.

Jesus described Himself as the "one who is holy and true, the one who has the key of David. What he opens, no one can close; and what he closes, no one can open" (Revelation 3:7). Because only God is holy (Isaiah 6:3), Jesus as the "one who is holy" is here pictured as God (compare with Mark 1:24; Luke 4:34; John 6:69). Jesus is also called the one who is "true." Unlike the false gods of paganism (such as Dionysus), Jesus was genuinely God.

Jesus also possessed "the key of David." That is, He had the authority to open and shut the door that leads into the prophesied Davidic kingdom—Christ's millennial kingdom (see Isaiah 22:22; Matthew 1:1).

Jesus informed the church at Philadelphia, "I know all the things you do" (Revelation 3:8). We again recall that Jesus was described as having eyes "like flames of fire" (1:14)—pointing to His ability to see all things as they truly are. He is able to accurately diagnose both the strengths and weaknesses of the seven churches.

Jesus then gave a glowing commendation to the church:

> I have opened a door for you that no one can close. You have little strength, yet you obeyed my word and did not deny me. Look, I will force those who belong to Satan's synagogue—those liars who say they are Jews but are not— to come and bow down at your feet. They will acknowledge that you are the ones I love (Revelation 3:8-9).

This means that Jesus sovereignly gave the church at Philadelphia an opportunity to serve in ministry, and no human had the ability to thwart that (see Acts 16:6-10). Though the church had little strength, God's strength was more than able to make up for human weakness (see 2 Corinthians 12:9).

Jesus's comment about the synagogue of Satan refers to people who were Jews by lineage—that is, they were descendants of Abraham—yet had rejected Jesus Christ (see John 8:31-59). In doing this, they became tools of Satan. It is likely that these Jews tried to force church members to deny Christ's name. But the believers stood firm. Eventually these Jewish antagonists would be forced to admit their error—perhaps at the great white throne judgment (Revelation 20:11-15). Contrary to Jewish exclusivism, it will become clear to all that God loved these Gentile believers who had been faithful to Jesus.

We now come upon one of the most important prophetic promises found in the book of Revelation: "Because you have obeyed my command to persevere, I will protect you from the great time of testing that will come upon the whole world to test those who belong to this world" (Revelation 3:10). This "great time of testing" is apparently a reference to the future seven-year tribulation period. This period of trial is described in detail in Revelation 4–19. It is from this period of trial that the church is to be kept.

Contextually, this promise looks far beyond the church of Philadelphia. Indeed, our text later says, "Anyone with ears to hear must listen to the Spirit and understand what he is saying *to the churches*" (Revelation 3:13). The reference "to the churches" greatly broadens the scope of the promise.

Now let's unpack some of the finer details of the verse. Notice that the church was to be kept from the *actual time period of testing* that would come upon the earth. It is not as though God will protect His people while they are *in* the tribulation period. Rather, they will be kept *from* the time period itself, and this will take place via the rapture of the church. The rapture is that glorious event in which the dead in Christ will be resurrected and living Christians will be instantly translated into their resurrection bodies—and both groups will be caught up to meet Christ in the air. From there, He will take them to heaven (John 14:1-3; 1 Corinthians 15:51-54; 1 Thessalonians 4:13-17).

I don't want to get too technical, but the Greek preposition *ek* that is translated "from" ("I will protect you *from* the great time of testing") carries the idea of separation from something. Believers will be kept from the hour of testing in the sense that they will be *completely separated* from it by being raptured before the period even begins. This makes sense, because Scripture elsewhere tells us that the church is to be delivered from the wrath to come (Romans 5:9; 1 Thessalonians 1:9-10; 5:9).

Renald Showers, in his helpful book *Maranatha: Our Lord Come!*, suggests that

> the language in Jesus's reference to this future period of worldwide testing implied that it was well-known to the

church saints. It was well-known because both Old and New Testament Scriptures, written years before Revelation, foretold this unique, future period of testing or Tribulation, which would take place prior to the coming of the Messiah to rule the world in the Messianic Age or Millennium (Isa. 2:10-21; Dan. 12:1; Zeph. 1:14-18; Mt. 24:4-31).[1]

Of course, Revelation 3:10 promises only that church saints will be kept out of this hour of trial coming upon the entire earth. Those who become believers *during* the hour of trial itself (what we might call tribulation saints) will go through tribulation. Arnold Fruchtenbaum has this clarifying comment in his book *The Footsteps of the Messiah*:

> Throughout the Tribulation, saints are being killed on a massive scale (Rev. 6:9-11; 11:7; 12:11; 13:7, 15; 14:13; 17:6; 18:24). If these saints are Church saints, they are not being kept safe and Revelation 3:10 is meaningless. Only if Church saints and Tribulation saints are kept distinct does the promise of Revelation 3:10 make any sense.[2]

In keeping with the idea that the church will be raptured before this time of tribulation begins, no Old Testament passage on the tribulation mentions the church (Deuteronomy 4:29-30; Jeremiah 30:4-11; Daniel 8:24-27; 12:1-2). Likewise, no New Testament passage on the tribulation mentions the church (Matthew 13:30,39-42,48-50; 24:15-31; 1 Thessalonians 1:9-10; 5:4-9; 2 Thessalonians 2:1-11; Revelation 4–18). The church's complete absence in these passages would seem to indicate that it is not on earth during the tribulation.

It is highly revealing that all throughout Scripture God is seen protecting His people before judgment falls (see 2 Peter 2:5-9). Enoch was transferred to heaven before the judgment of the flood. Noah and his family were in the ark before the arrival of the flood. Lot was taken out of Sodom before judgment was poured out on Sodom and Gomorrah. The firstborn among the Hebrews in Egypt were sheltered by the blood of the Paschal lamb before judgment fell. The spies were safely out of Jericho and Rahab was secured before judgment fell on Jericho. So, too, the church will be secured safely (via the rapture) before judgment falls during the tribulation period.

Scripture reveals that the rapture is *imminent*—that is, there are no prophecies that need to be fulfilled before the rapture occurs (1 Corinthians 1:7; 16:22; Philippians 3:20; 4:5; 1 Thessalonians 1:10; Titus 2:13; Hebrews 9:28; James 5:7-9; 1 Peter 1:13; Jude 21). This fact ought to motivate us to live in righteousness and purity (Romans 13:11-14; 2 Peter 3:10-14; 1 John 3:2-3).

This is why Jesus told the Philadelphian Christians, "I am coming soon. Hold on to what you have, so that no one will take away your crown" (Revelation 3:11). Because we do not know when the rapture will occur, we must always be ready, living in holiness (Titus 2:13-14).

All who are victorious—those who are faithful and obedient— "will become pillars in the Temple of my God, and they will never have to leave it. And I will write on them the name of my God, and they will be citizens in the city of my God—the new Jerusalem that comes down from heaven from my God. And I will also write on them my new name" (Revelation 3:12).

The "pillar" imagery is significant. In Bible times, magistrates were honored in Philadelphia by having a pillar placed within a temple in their name. Here, Jesus indicated that faithful believers would be so honored (see Revelation 21:22). In contrast to earthly temples, in which pillars eventually decay and fall over, believers will continue forever in the temple in heaven—the New Jerusalem.

Jesus indicated He would write the name of God on His followers (Revelation 3:12). In Bible times, imprinting a name on something indicated ownership. God's writing of His name on Christians identifies them as belonging to Him, as being His redeemed property, as being in His eternal family.

Jesus promised that His people "will be citizens in the city of my God—the new Jerusalem." The New Jerusalem is the heavenly city in which the saints of all ages will eternally dwell (see Hebrews 11:10; John 14:1-3; Revelation 3:12). The most elaborate description of this city appears in Revelation 21. Presented to our amazed gaze is a scene of such transcendent splendor that the human mind can scarcely take it in. This is a scene of ecstatic joy and fellowship of sinless angels and redeemed glorified human beings. The voice of the one identified as the Alpha and the Omega, the beginning and the end, utters a climactic declaration: "Look, I am making everything new!" (Revelation 21:5).

As was true with the previous churches, Christ's closing words to the church at Philadelphia urge obedience to these prophetic revelations inspired by the Holy Spirit (2 Timothy 3:15-17; 2 Peter 1:21).

To the Church in Laodicea

The final church to receive evaluative comments from Christ was the church at Laodicea, a wealthy and commercially successful city that was east of Ephesus, west of Colossae. Its three primary industries were banking (gold), clothing (wool), and medicine (eye salve). Because the city struggled with an inadequate water supply, an underground aqueduct was built so that water could be piped in from hot springs south of the city. This hot water became lukewarm as it made its way to Laodicea.

Christ described Himself as "the one who is the Amen—the faithful and true witness, the beginning of God's new creation" (Revelation 3:14). In Isaiah 65:16, there is a reference to the "God of truth," which in Hebrew translates to the "God of amen." This title used of God in the Old Testament was applied to Jesus in Revelation 3:14, for Christ Himself is the God of truth. As the God of truth, here He tells the truth about the condition of the church of Laodicea. Honesty is the first step in correcting a problem. That Jesus is a faithful and true witness indicates that He is a reliable source of the revelation being set forth to the church (see John 14:6).

What does Jesus mean when He refers to Himself as "the beginning of God's new creation"? There is a wide range of meanings for the Greek word *arche*, translated "beginning" in Revelation 3:14. Though *arche* can mean "beginning," the word also carries the important meaning of "one who begins," "origin," "source," "creator," or "first cause." This is the intended meaning of the word in Revelation 3:14—Jesus is the Creator or First Cause of the creation. Note that the English word *architect* is derived from *arche*. We might say that Jesus is the architect of all creation (see John 1:3; Colossians 1:16; Hebrews 1:2).

Greek scholars note that another possible meaning of *arche* is "ruler" or "magistrate." These scholars observe that when *arche* is used of a person in Scripture, it is almost always used of a ruler (see Romans 8:38; Ephesians 3:10; Colossians 2:15).

The English word *archbishop* is related to this sense of the Greek word *arche*. An archbishop is one who is in authority over other bishops. If "ruler" is the correct meaning for *arche* in Revelation 3:14, then it means that Christ has authority over all creation.

It seems likely that in the case of Christ, both senses are intended inasmuch as Christ is elsewhere portrayed in Scripture as both the Creator (Hebrews 1:2) and Ruler (Revelation 19:16) of all things.

Jesus then said to the church at Laodicea, "I know all the things you do" (Revelation 3:15). Christ sees all things as they truly are. He thus accurately diagnoses both the strengths and weaknesses of the church at Laodicea.

The church must have dreaded hearing Christ's assessment: "You are neither hot nor cold. I wish that you were one or the other! But since you are like lukewarm water, neither hot nor cold, I will spit you out of my mouth!" (verses 15-16).

This is an allusion to the underground aqueduct mentioned earlier—in which the water became lukewarm in transit to Laodicea. The situation at Laodicea was in contrast to the hot springs in nearby Hieropolis and the pure, cold water in nearby Colossae.

Just as a resident of Laodicea recognized that the water was neither cold nor hot, so Christ recognized that church members were neither cold nor hot. The church at Laodicea was not spiritually dead, but neither was it filled with spiritual zeal. Church members were neutral and even compromising. This needed to be rectified.

Just as a person might be tempted to spit out the dirty, tepid water of Laodicea, so Christ wanted to spew out these lukewarm church members. A neutral or compromising attitude was unacceptable to Him. He thus called for complete obedience and commitment. Partial obedience would not suffice. "Spitting out of the mouth" is apparently a graphic metaphor representing divine discipline.

Jesus then continued His dire assessment of the church: "You say, 'I am rich. I have everything I want. I don't need a thing!' And you don't realize that you are wretched and miserable and poor and blind and naked" (Revelation 3:17).

Because of the three primary industries of the city—which had to do with gold, clothing, and eye salve—people in the city were quite wealthy. They had nice homes, nice clothes, and were affluent. This outward wealth led the church to a state of spiritual complacency. Church members were so enamored with material things that they were blind to their true condition. Words like "wretched" and "miserable" paint a sad picture of the spiritual state of this church.

Scripture elsewhere reveals that a love of money and riches can lead to destruction. The apostle Paul stated that "people who long to be rich fall into temptation and are trapped by many foolish and harmful desires that plunge them into ruin and destruction" (1 Timothy 6:9). Jesus warned His followers, "Beware! Guard against every kind of greed. Life is not measured by how much you own" (Luke 12:15). He urged that believers have an eternal perspective, laying up treasures in heaven instead of on earth (Matthew 6:19-20).

Jesus then suggested a remedy to the church at Laodicea: "I advise you to buy gold from me—gold that has been purified by fire. Then you will be rich. Also buy white garments from me so you will not be shamed by your nakedness, and ointment for your eyes so you will be able to see" (Revelation 3:18). The Lord here alludes to the city's three main sources of income: banking, the production of wool cloth, and medicine. Jesus was speaking in terms they would understand. In the process, He drew a powerful contrast. Because the Laodiceans were wealthy, they were blind to their spiritual impoverishment. Because they had expensive garments on their bodies, they were blind to their spiritual nakedness. Even though good eyesight was made possible by their production of eye salve, they were unaware of their spiritual blindness. For these reasons, Christ called the church to repentance.

Christ is a Lord who disciplines His people: "I correct and discipline everyone I love. So be diligent and turn from your indifference" (Revelation 3:19). If a child of God sins and refuses to repent, God brings discipline—which can sometimes be very severe—into his or her life to bring them to repentance (Proverbs 3:11-12; Hebrews 12:4-11). Christians will either respond to God's *light* or they will respond to His *heat*.

When Christ urged His people to "be diligent," He used a present imperative in the original Greek text. The imperative indicates that this is a command and not a mere option. The present tense indicates that the action is to be ongoing. We might paraphrase this, "*Keep on* being diligent, moment by moment, day by day."

The phrase "turn from your indifference" is literally "repent at once." As noted earlier, the word *repent* means to change one's thinking with a subsequent change in behavior. These church members needed to turn immediately from their wrong thinking and behavior.

Christ then gave one of the most amazing appeals in all of Scripture: "Look! I stand at the door and knock. If you hear my voice and open the door, I will come in, and we will share a meal together as friends" (Revelation 3:20). These words were directed at a church. It is tragic that Christ had to rebuke the people in this church for excluding Him from their lives. He sought intimate fellowship with them, and took the initiative to restore that fellowship by knocking at their hearts.

The faithful and obedient are given a wonderful promise: "Those who are victorious will sit with me on my throne, just as I was victorious and sat with my Father on his throne" (Revelation 3:21). Scripture promises that Christ will one day reign from the Davidic throne (2 Samuel 7:12-13), and that the faithful will reign with Him. In 2 Timothy 2:12, for example, Paul wrote, "If we endure hardship, we will reign with him." Those who persevere through trials will one day rule with Christ in His future kingdom.

There is an interesting parallel between Jesus Christ and Christians here. After all, Christ Himself endured and will one day reign (1 Corinthians 15:25). In the same way—though obviously to a much lesser degree, and under the lordship of Christ—believers must endure and will one day reign with Him (Revelation 3:21).

That we will reign with Christ is confirmed elsewhere in the book of Revelation. For example, Revelation 5:10 reveals that believers have been made "a Kingdom of priests for our God. And they will reign on the earth." Likewise, Revelation 20:6 affirms, "Blessed and holy are those who share in the first resurrection. For them the second death holds no power, but they will be priests of God and of Christ and will reign with him a thousand years."

This privilege of reigning with Christ will continue even beyond the millennial kingdom. Revelation 22:5 says of the eternal state (which follows the millennial kingdom), "There will be no night there—no need for lamps or sun—for the Lord God will shine on them. And they will reign forever and ever." What an awesome privilege and blessing we have awaiting us!

Christ closed by urging the church members at Laodicea to hear and obey what the Spirit has communicated to them. It is not enough to merely hear; one must obey.

Life Lessons from the Seven Churches

As we close, let us review the primary lessons we learn from Christ's words to the seven churches:

- Doctrinal accuracy and moral purity are very important, but these things are not enough. Supreme love for God and others is also necessary. Christianity is more than just being doctrinally correct. It involves an ongoing love relationship with the Lord.

- Don't sweat over earthly troubles. Our destiny in heaven is secure. Rejoice!

- Repent of openness to false teachings, which can lead to inappropriate behavior.

- Abstain from—*flee* from—all forms of fornication.

- Avoid hypocrisy, which involves the pretense of having a virtuous character when in reality no such virtue is present.

- Don't be lukewarm in your commitment to God.

Let's choose to hear and obey.

Postscript:
You Can Trust Biblical Prophecy

From the book of Genesis to the book of Malachi, the Old Testament abounds with anticipations of the first coming of the Messiah. Numerous predictions—fulfilled to the "crossing of the t" and the "dotting of the i" in the New Testament—relate to Christ's birth, life, ministry, death, resurrection, and glory.

Some liberal scholars have attempted to argue that these prophecies were given after Jesus lived, not before. They have suggested that the books of the Old Testament were written close to the time of Christ and that the messianic prophecies were merely Christian inventions. But to make such a claim is to completely ignore the historical evidence. Bible scholars Norman Geisler and Ron Brooks point out:

> Even the most liberal critics admit that the prophetic books were completed some 400 years before Christ, and the Book of Daniel by about 167 BC. Though there is good evidence to date most of these books much earlier (some of the psalms and earlier prophets were in the eighth and ninth centuries BC), what difference would it make? It is just as hard to predict an event 200 years in the future as it is to predict one that is 800 years in the future. Both feats would require nothing less than divine knowledge.[1]

God's ability to foretell future events confirms that He alone is God, and separates Him from all the false gods of this world. Addressing the polytheism of Isaiah's time, God said,

> Who is like me? Let him proclaim it. Let him declare and set it before me, since I appointed an ancient people. Let them declare what is to come, and what will happen (Isaiah 44:7 ESV).

> Declare and present your case; let them take counsel together! Who told this long ago? Who declared it of old? Was it not I, the LORD? And there is no other god besides me, a righteous God and a Savior; there is none besides me (Isaiah 45:21 ESV).

> The former things I declared of old; they went out from my mouth, and I announced them; then suddenly I did them, and they came to pass…I declared them to you from of old, before they came to pass I announced them to you, lest you should say, "My idol did them, my carved image and my metal image commanded them" (Isaiah 48:3,5 ESV).

Of course, anyone can make predictions—that is easy. But having them fulfilled is another story altogether. "The more statements you make about the future and the greater the detail, the better the chances are that you will be proven wrong."[2] But God was never wrong; all the messianic prophecies of the first coming in the Old Testament were fulfilled specifically and precisely in the person of Jesus Christ.

Jesus often indicated to listeners that He was the specific fulfillment of messianic prophecy. For example, He made the following comments on different occasions:

- "Do not think that I have come to abolish the Law or the Prophets; I have not come to abolish them but to fulfill them" (Matthew 5:17 ESV).

- "All this has taken place that the Scriptures of the prophets might be fulfilled" (Matthew 26:56 ESV).

- "Beginning with Moses and all the Prophets, he interpreted to them in all the Scriptures the things concerning himself" (Luke 24:27 ESV).

- "These are my words that I spoke to you while I was still with you, that everything written about me in the Law of Moses and the Prophets and the Psalms must be fulfilled" (Luke 24:44 ESV).

- "You search the Scriptures because you think that in them you have eternal life; and it is they that bear witness about me, yet you refuse to come to me that you may have life" (John 5:39-40 ESV).

- "If you believed Moses, you would believe me; for he wrote of me. But if you do not believe his writings, how will you believe my words?" (John 5:46-47 ESV).

- "He rolled up the scroll and gave it back to the attendant and sat down. And the eyes of all in the synagogue were fixed on him. And he began to say to them, 'Today this Scripture has been fulfilled in your hearing'" (Luke 4:20-21 ESV).

An in-depth study of the messianic prophecies in the Old Testament is beyond the scope of this postscript. However, the chart below lists some of the more important messianic prophecies that were fulfilled by Jesus Christ:

	Old Testament Prophecy	New Testament Fulfillment in Christ
Seed of woman	Genesis 3:15	Galatians 4:4
Line of Abraham	Genesis 12:2	Matthew 1:1
Line of Jacob	Numbers 24:17	Luke 3:23,34
Line of Judah	Genesis 49:10	Matthew 1:2

Line of Jesse	Isaiah 11:1	Luke 3:23,32
Line of David	2 Samuel 7:12-16	Matthew 1:1
Virgin birth	Isaiah 7:14	Matthew 1:23
Birthplace: Bethlehem	Micah 5:2	Matthew 2:6
Forerunner: John	Isaiah 40:3; Malachi 3:1	Matthew 3:3
Escape into Egypt	Hosea 11:1	Matthew 2:14
Herod kills children	Jeremiah 31:15	Matthew 2:16
King	Psalm 2:6	Matthew 21:5
Prophet	Deuteronomy 18:15-18	Acts 3:22-23
Priest	Psalm 110:4	Hebrews 5:6-10
Judge	Isaiah 33:22	John 5:30
Called "Lord"	Psalm 110:1	Luke 2:11
Called "Immanuel"	Isaiah 7:14	Matthew 1:23
Anointed by Holy Spirit	Isaiah 11:2	Matthew 3:16-17
Zeal for God	Psalm 69:9	John 2:15-17
Ministry in Galilee	Isaiah 9:1-2	Matthew 4:12-16
Ministry of miracles	Isaiah 35:5-6	Matthew 9:35
Bore world's sins	Psalm 22:1	Matthew 27:46
Ridiculed	Psalm 22:7-8	Matthew 27:39,43
Stumbling stone to Jew	Psalm 118:22	1 Peter 2:7
Rejected by own people	Isaiah 53:3	John 7:5,48
Light to Gentiles	Isaiah 60:3	Acts 13:47-48
Taught parables	Psalm 78:2	Matthew 13:34
Cleansed the temple	Malachi 3:1	Matthew 21:12
Sold for 30 shekels	Zechariah 11:12	Matthew 26:15
Forsaken by disciples	Zechariah 13:7	Mark 14:50

Silent before accusers	Isaiah 53:7	Matthew 27:12-19
Hands and feet pierced	Psalm 22:16	John 20:25
Heart broken	Psalm 22:14	John 19:34
Crucified with thieves	Isaiah 53:12	Matthew 27:38
No bones broken	Psalm 22:17	John 19:33-36
Soldiers gambled	Psalm 22:18	John 19:24
Suffered thirst on cross	Psalm 69:21	John 19:28
Vinegar offered	Psalm 69:21	Matthew 27:34
Christ's prayer	Psalm 22:24	Matthew 26:39
Disfigured	Isaiah 52:14	John 19:1
Scourging and death	Isaiah 53:5	John 19:1,18
His "forsaken" cry	Psalm 22:1	Matthew 27:46
Committed self to God	Psalm 31:5	Luke 23:46
Rich man's tomb	Isaiah 53:9	Matthew 27:57-60
Resurrection	Psalm 16:10; 22:22	Matthew 28:6
Ascension	Psalm 68:18	Luke 24:50-53
Right hand of God	Psalm 110:1	Hebrews 1:3

Any reasonable person who examines these Old Testament prophecies in an objective manner must conclude that Jesus was indeed the promised Messiah. *These prophecies were literally and specifically fulfilled in Him.* And herein lies the point I wish to make.

The precedent for interpreting Bible prophecy is found in the prophecies of the first coming of Jesus Christ. More than 100 messianic prophecies were *literally fulfilled* in Christ's first coming. Likewise, the prophecies relating to the second coming (and the events that lead up to it, as well as the events that follow it) will be fulfilled literally as well. This is why I like to tell people that *if you want to understand how God is going to fulfill prophecy in the future, take a look at how He has fulfilled prophecy in the past.*

This means we can take Jesus's many prophecies of the future in a literal fashion. Based on Jesus's prophecies, we can rest assured that the following future events will indeed come to pass:

- Christ's preparation of a place for us in heaven
- The rapture of the church
- The tribulation period
- The rise of false Christs
- Wars and threats of wars
- Famines
- Earthquakes
- Persecution of God's people
- Martyrdom
- Pervasive death
- Global apostasy
- The gospel preached to all nations
- The defiling of the future Jewish temple
- God's preservation of a Jewish remnant during the tribulation period
- Counterfeit signs and wonders
- Cosmic disturbances
- Specific judgments that fall during the tribulation period
- The necessity of being ready for the Lord's coming
- A series of "signs of the times" preceding the second coming
- Pervasive carousing and ignoring those who preach God's Word
- The second coming in glory

- The establishment of the millennial kingdom
- God's fulfillment of Old Testament promises to Israel in the millennial kingdom
- The final judgment
- Resurrection
- The eternal state (heaven and hell)

As I close, I want to urge you not only to continue studying what Scripture says about the prophetic future, but also to keep your eyes focused on heaven (Colossians 3:1-2). Every single day that passes brings you one day nearer to the rapture, after which you'll immediately be taken to heaven, never again to be separated from your beloved Lord and Savior, Jesus Christ. The day of your redemption draws ever nearer.

Come soon, Lord!

Appendixes

Appendix A:
If You Are Not a Christian...

Saying yes to a personal relationship with Jesus is the most important decision you could ever make in your life. It is unlike any other relationship. If you go into eternity without this relationship, you will spend eternity apart from Him.

If you will allow me, I would like to tell you how you can come into a personal relationship with Jesus.

First you need to recognize that...

God Desires a Personal Relationship with You

God created you (Genesis 1:27). And He did not create you to exist all alone and apart from Him. He created you with a view to coming into a personal relationship with Him.

God has fellowshipped with His people throughout Bible times (for example, Genesis 3:8-19). Just as God fellowshipped with them, so He desires to fellowship with you (1 John 1:5-7). God loves you (John 3:16). Never forget that fact.

The problem is...

Humanity Has a Sin Problem that Blocks a Relationship with God

When Adam and Eve chose to sin against God in the Garden of Eden, they catapulted the entire human race—to which they gave birth—into sin. Since that time, every human being has been born into the world with a propensity to sin.

The apostle Paul affirmed that "when Adam sinned, sin entered the world. Adam's sin brought death, so death spread to everyone" (Romans 5:12). We are told that "because one person disobeyed God, many became sinners" (Romans 5:19). Ultimately this means that "death came into the world through a man" (Adam), and "everyone dies because we all belong to Adam" (1 Corinthians 15:21-22).

Jesus often spoke of sin in metaphors that illustrate the havoc sin can wreak in one's life. He described sin as blindness (Matthew 23:16-26), sickness (Matthew 9:12), being enslaved in bondage (John 8:34), and living in darkness (John 8:12; 12:35-46). Moreover, Jesus taught that this is a universal condition and that all people are guilty before God (Luke 7:37-48).

Jesus also taught that both inner thoughts and external acts render a person guilty (Matthew 5:28). He taught that from within the human heart come evil thoughts, sexual immorality, theft, murder, adultery, greed, malice, deceit, envy, slander, arrogance, and folly (Mark 7:21-23). Moreover, He affirmed that God is fully aware of every person's sins, both external acts and inner thoughts; nothing escapes His notice (Matthew 22:18; Luke 6:8; John 4:17-19).

Of course, some people are more morally upright than others. However, we all fall short of God's infinite standards (Romans 3:23). In a contest to see who can throw a rock to the moon, I am sure a muscular athlete would be able to throw it much farther than I could. But all human beings ultimately fall short of the task. Similarly, all of us fall short of measuring up to God's perfect holy standards.

Though the sin problem is a serious one, God has graciously provided a solution:

Jesus Died for Our Sins and Made Salvation Possible

God's absolute holiness demands that sin be punished. The good news of the gospel, however, is that Jesus has taken this punishment on Himself. God loves us so much that He sent Jesus to bear the penalty for our sins!

Jesus affirmed that it was for the very purpose of dying that He came into the world (John 12:27). Moreover, He perceived His death as being a sacrificial offering for the sins of humanity (Matthew 26:26-28). Jesus took His sacrificial mission with utmost seriousness, for He knew that without Him, humanity would certainly perish (Matthew 16:25; John 3:16) and spend eternity apart from God in a place of great suffering (Matthew 10:28; 11:23; 23:33; 25:41; Luke 16:22-28).

Jesus therefore described His mission this way: "The Son of Man came not to be served but to serve others and to give his life as a ransom for many" (Matthew 20:28). "The Son of Man came to seek and save those who are lost" (Luke 19:10). "God sent his Son into the world not to judge the world, but to save the world through him" (John 3:17).

Please be aware that the benefits of Christ's death on the cross are not automatically applied to your life. *To receive the gift of salvation, you must...*

Believe in Jesus Christ the Savior

By His sacrificial death on the cross, Jesus took the sins of the entire world on Himself and made salvation available for everyone (1 John 2:2). But this salvation is not automatic. Only those who personally choose to believe in Christ are saved. This is the consistent testimony of the biblical Jesus. Listen to His words:

- "This is how God loved the world: He gave his one and only Son, so that everyone who believes in him will not perish but have eternal life" (John 3:16).
- "It is my Father's will that all who see his Son and believe in him should have eternal life. I will raise them up at the last day" (John 6:40).

- "I am the resurrection and the life. Anyone who believes in me will live, even after dying" (John 11:25).

Choosing *not* to believe in Jesus, by contrast, leads to eternal condemnation: "There is no judgment against anyone who believes in him. But anyone who does not believe in him has already been judged for not believing in God's one and only Son" (John 3:18).

Free at Last: Forgiven of All Sins

When you believe in Christ the Savior, a wonderful thing happens. God forgives you of all your sins. All of them! He puts them completely out of His sight. Ponder for a few minutes the following verses, which speak of the forgiveness of those who have believed in Christ:

- "He is so rich in kindness and grace that he purchased our freedom with the blood of his Son and forgave our sins" (Ephesians 1:7).
- God said, "I will never again remember their sins and lawless deeds" (Hebrews 10:17).
- "Oh, what joy for those whose disobedience is forgiven, whose sin is put out of sight! Yes, what joy for those whose record the LORD has cleared of guilt, whose lives are lived in complete honesty!" (Psalm 32:1-2).
- "His unfailing love toward those who fear him is as great as the height of the heavens above the earth. He has removed our sins as far from us as the east is from the west" (Psalm 103:11-12).

Such forgiveness is wonderful indeed, for none of us can possibly work our way into heaven, or be good enough to warrant God's good favor. Because of what Jesus has done for us, we can freely receive the gift of salvation. It is a gift provided solely through the grace of God (Ephesians 2:8-9). It becomes ours by placing our faith in Jesus.

Don't Put It Off

It is a dangerous thing to put off turning to Christ for salvation, for you do not know the day of your death. What if it happens this evening? "Everyone dies—so the living should take this to heart" (Ecclesiastes 7:2).

If God is speaking to your heart now, then now is your door of opportunity to believe. "Seek the Lord while you can find him. Call on him now while he is near" (Isaiah 55:6).

Follow Me in Prayer

Would you like to place your faith in Jesus for the forgiveness of sins, thereby guaranteeing your eternal place in heaven along His side? If so, pray the following prayer with me.

Keep in mind that it is not the prayer itself that saves you. It is the faith in your heart that saves you. So let the following prayer be a simple expression of the faith that is in your heart:

> *Dear Jesus:*
> *I want to have a relationship with You.*
> *I know I cannot save myself, because I know I am a sinner.*
> *Thank You for dying on the cross on my behalf.*
> *I believe You died for me, and I accept Your free gift of salvation.*
> *Thank You, Jesus.*
> *Amen.*

Welcome to God's Forever Family

On the authority of the Word of God, I can now assure you that you are a part of God's forever family. If you prayed the above prayer with a heart of faith, you will spend all eternity by the side of Jesus in heaven. Welcome to God's family!

What to Do Next

1. Purchase a Bible and read from it daily. Read at least one chapter a day, followed by a time of prayer. If you've not read the Bible before, I recommend that you obtain an easy translation—such as the New Living Translation (NLT). I also recommend starting with the Gospel of Luke.

2. Join a Bible-believing church immediately. Get involved in it. Join a Bible study group at the church so you will have regular fellowship with other Christians.

3. Send me an email at ronrhodes@earthlink.net. I would love to hear from you if you have made a decision for Christ.

Appendix B:
Scripture Index of
Jesus's Prophecies

Abomination of desolation—Matthew 24:15

Angels will gather people—Matthew 24:31

Be ready—Matthew 24:43-51

Betrayal and hatred—Matthew 24:10

Bridegroom metaphor and the rapture—John 14:1-3

Builds the New Jerusalem—John 14:2

Christ coming in clouds of glory—Matthew 24:30

Christ's prophetic words a sure thing—Matthew 24:35

Cosmic disturbances in the end times—Matthew 24:29

Counterfeit signs and wonders—Matthew 24:24

Day or hour, no one knows—Matthew 24:36

Days of Noah, like the—Matthew 24:37-39

Earthquakes—Matthew 24:7

False Christs—Matthew 24:4-5,23,26

False prophets—Matthew 24:11,24

Famines—Matthew 24:7

Second coming—Matthew 24:27,30

Sign of the Son of Man—Matthew 24:30

Signs indicate that the end is near—Matthew 24:28

Sin rampant—Matthew 24:12

Tribulation shortened for human survival—Matthew 24:22

Turning from Christ—Matthew 24:10

Two men working, two women grinding—Matthew 24:40

Unpreparedness for Lord's coming—Matthew 24:39

Wars and rumors of wars—Matthew 24:6

Bibliography

Ankerberg, John, and Dillon Burroughs. *Middle East Meltdown*. Eugene, OR: Harvest House, 2007.

Fruchtenbaum, Arnold. *The Footsteps of the Messiah*. San Antonio, TX: Ariel, 2004.

Geisler, Norman. *Systematic Theology: Church/Last Things*, vol. 4. St. Paul, MN: Bethany House, 2005.

Hays, J. Daniel, J. Scott Duvall, and C. Marvin Pate. *Dictionary of Biblical Prophecy and End Times*. Grand Rapids, MI: Zondervan, 2007.

Hitchcock, Mark. *Bible Prophecy*. Wheaton, IL: Tyndale, 1999.

———. *Iran: The Coming Crisis*. Sisters, OR: Multnomah, 2006.

———. *Is America in Bible Prophecy?* Sisters, OR: Multnomah, 2002.

———. *The Coming Islamic Invasion of Israel*. Sisters, OR: Multnomah, 2002.

———. *The Late Great United States*. Colorado Springs, CO: Multnomah, 2009.

———. *The Second Coming of Babylon*. Sisters, OR: Multnomah, 2003.

Hoyt, Herman. *The End Times*. Chicago, IL: Moody, 1969.

Ice, Thomas, and Randall Price. *Ready to Rebuild: The Imminent Plan to Rebuild the Last Days Temple*. Eugene, OR: Harvest House, 1992.

Ice, Thomas, and Timothy Demy. *Prophecy Watch*. Eugene, OR: Harvest House, 1998.

———. *What the Bible Says About Heaven and Eternity*. Grand Rapids, MI: Kregel, 2000.

———. *When the Trumpet Sounds*. Eugene, OR: Harvest House, 1995.

LaHaye, Tim. *The Beginning of the End*. Wheaton, IL: Tyndale, 1991.

———. *The Coming Peace in the Middle East*. Grand Rapids, MI: Zondervan, 1984.

LaHaye, Tim, and Jerry Jenkins. *Are We Living in the End Times?* Wheaton, IL: Tyndale, 1999.

LaHaye, Tim, and Thomas Ice. *Charting the End Times*. Eugene, OR: Harvest House, 2001.

Pentecost, J. Dwight. *The Words and Works of Jesus Christ*. Grand Rapids, MI: Zondervan, 1978.

———. *Things to Come*. Grand Rapids, MI: Zondervan, 1964.

Price, Randall. *Fast Facts on the Middle East Conflict*. Eugene, OR: Harvest House, 2003.

———. *Unholy War*. Eugene, OR: Harvest House, 2001.

Prophecy Study Bible, ed. Tim LaHaye. Chattanooga, TN: AMG, 2001.

Rosenberg, Joel. *Epicenter: Why Current Rumblings in the Middle East Will Change Your Future*. Carol Stream, IL: Tyndale, 2006.

Ryrie, Charles. *Dispensationalism Today*. Chicago, IL: Moody, 1965.

Showers, Renald. *Maranatha: Our Lord Come!* Bellmawr, NJ: The Friends of Israel Gospel Ministry, 1995.

The MacArthur Study Bible, ed. John MacArthur. Nashville, TN: Thomas Nelson, 2003.

The Popular Bible Prophecy Commentary, eds. Tim LaHaye and Ed Hindson. Eugene, OR: Harvest House, 2006.

The Popular Encyclopedia of Bible Prophecy, eds. Tim LaHaye and Ed Hindson. Eugene, OR: Harvest House, 2004.

The Ryrie Study Bible, ed. Charles Ryrie. Chicago, IL: Moody, 2011.

Toussaint, Stanley. *Behold the King: A Study of Matthew*. Grand Rapids, MI: Kregel, 2005.

Unger, Merrill F. *Beyond the Crystal Ball*. Chicago, IL: Moody, 1978.

Walvoord, John. *Jesus Christ Our Lord*. Chicago, IL: Moody, 1980.

———. *End Times*. Nashville, TN: Word, 1998.

———. *Matthew*. Chicago, IL: Moody, 2013.

———. *The Millennial Kingdom*. Grand Rapids, MI: Zondervan, 1975.

————. *The Prophecy Knowledge Handbook*. Wheaton, IL: Victor, 1990.

————. *The Return of the Lord*. Grand Rapids, MI: Zondervan, 1979.

Walvoord, John F., and John E. Walvoord. *Armageddon, Oil, and the Middle East Crisis*. Grand Rapids, MI: Zondervan, 1975.

Walvoord, John F., and Mark Hitchcock. *Armageddon, Oil, and Terror*. Carol Stream, IL: Tyndale, 2007.

Endnotes

Introduction: Jesus and the End Times

1. Thomas Schultz, quoted in Josh McDowell and Bart Larson, *Jesus: A Biblical Defense of His Deity* (San Bernardino, CA: Here's Life, 1983), 54.

2. Robert L. Reymond, "God as Trinity," article posted at http://learntheology.com/god_trinity.html, based on *A New Systematic Theology of the Christian Faith* (Nashville, TN: Thomas Nelson, 1998).

3. John F. Walvoord, *Jesus Christ Our Lord* (Chicago, IL: Moody, 1980), 254-55.

4. See, for example, Robert L. Reymond, *Jesus, Divine Messiah: The Old Testament Witness* (Scotland: Christian Focus Publications, 1990), 101.

5. Quoted in Robert Jamieson, A.R. Fausset, and David Brown, *The Bethany Parallel Commentary on the New Testament* (Minneapolis, MN: Bethany House, 1983), 1368; see also Erich Sauer, *From Eternity to Eternity* (Grand Rapids, MI: Eerdmans, 1979), 45.

6. Millard J. Erickson, *Christian Theology* (Grand Rapids, MI: Baker, 1987), 765.

7. R.C.H. Lenski, *First Peter* (Minneapolis, MN: Augsburg, 1961), 46.

Chapter 1—The Rapture

1. John F. Walvoord, *End Times* (Nashville, TN: Word, 1998), 218.

2. Henry M. Morris, *The Biblical Basis for Modern Science* (Grand Rapids, MI: Baker, 1984), 156.

3. Anne Graham Lotz, *Heaven: My Father's House* (Nashville, TN: Thomas Nelson, 2001), 49.

4. Renald Showers, *Maranatha: Our Lord Come!* (Bellmawr, NJ: Friends of Israel, 1995), 214.

5. Arnold Fruchtenbaum, *The Footsteps of the Messiah* (San Antonio, TX: Ariel Ministries, 2004), n.p.

Chapter 2—The Tribulation Period, Part 1

1. *The Believer's Bible Commentary*, in The Bible Study App, Olive Tree Software.

2. Thomas Constable, "Notes on Revelation," posted at soniclight.com.

3. William MacDonald and Arthur L. Farstad, *The Believer's Bible Commentary*, E-Sword Bible Software.

Chapter 3—The Tribulation Period, Part 2

1. Renald Showers, *Maranatha: Our Lord Come!* (Bellmawr, NJ: Friends of Israel, 1995), 43.

2. Showers, *Maranatha: Our Lord Come!*, 50.

3. Tim LaHaye and Ed Hindson, *Global Warning* (Eugene, OR: Harvest House, 2007), 192.

Chapter 4—Be Alert: The Parable of the Fig Tree

1. John MacArthur, *New Testament Commentary* (Chicago, IL: Moody, 1994), in Accordance, Oaktree Software.

2. Warren W. Wiersbe, *Wiersbe's Expository Outlines on the Old Testament and New Testament* (Colorado Springs, CO: David C. Cook, 1993), The Bible Study App, Olive Tree Software.

3. Harold L. Willmington, *The Outline Bible* (Wheaton, IL: Tyndale, 2000), in Logos Bible Software.

4. Lewis Sperry Chafer, *Chafer's Systematic Theology* (Dallas: Dallas Seminary Press, 1983), The Bible Study App, Olive Tree Software; insert added for clarification.

5. John F. Walvoord, *Every Prophecy in the Bible* (Colorado Springs, CO: David C. Cook, 1990), Kindle edition.

6. MacArthur, *New Testament Commentary*.

7. Thomas Constable, *Thomas Constable's Notes on the Bible* (CreateSpace, 2017), The Bible Study App, Olive Tree Software.

8. J. Dwight Pentecost, *The Parables of Jesus* (Grand Rapids, MI: Kregel, 1982), Kindle edition.

Chapter 5—Like the Days of Noah

1. Charles Berlitz, *Doomsday 1999 A.D.* (New York: Doubleday, 1981), 9.

2. Frederick H. Marten, *The Story of Human Life*, cited in *Critique*, vol. 31, 65.

3. Bill Lawren, "Are You Ready for Millennial Fever?," *Utne Reader*, March/April 1990; Stanley Young, "An Overview of the End," *Critique*, vol. 31 (1989): 28-31.

4. Most of the accounts of the turbulence and panic that accompanied the arrival of AD 1000 come indirectly from *Histories*, by Raoul Glaber, a Burgundian monk born in the late tenth century.

5. Russell Chandler, *Doomsday: The End of the World* (Ann Arbor, MI: Servant Publications, 1993), 54.

6. Chandler, *Doomsday*, 52.

7. Yuri Rubinsky and Ian Wiseman, *A History of the End of the World* (New York: William Morrow, 1982), 66.

8. Louis Berkhof, *The History of Christian Doctrines* (Grand Rapids, MI: Baker, 1981), 263.

9. Philip Schaff, *History of the Christian Church*, vol. 2 (n.p.: Arkose Press, 2015), 348.

10. Stanley J. Grenz, *The Millennial Maze: Sorting Out Evangelical Options* (Downers Grove, IL: InterVarsity, 1992), 14.

11. Grenz, *The Millennial Maze*, 44.

12. Henri Focillon, *The Year 1000* (New York: Frederick Ungar, n.d.), 59.

13. Focillon, *The Year 1000*, 60.

14. William Alnor, *Soothsayers of the Second Advent* (Grand Rapids, MI: Eerdmans, 1989), 31.

15. Alnor, *Soothsayers*, 33.

16. Alnor, *Soothsayers*, 29.

17. Alnor, *Soothsayers*, 31.

18. Cited by B.J. Oropeza, "One More End-Time Scare Ends with a Whimper," *Christian Research Journal*, Winter 1993, 6, 43.

19. Oropeza, "One More End-Time Scare," 43.

20. Oropeza, "One More End-Time Scare."

21. Oropeza, "One More End-Time Scare."

22. Perucci Ferraiuolo, "Could '1994' Be the End of Family Radio?," *Christian Research Journal*, Summer 1993, 5.

23. Ferraiuolo, "Could '1994' Be the End of Family Radio?," 5.

24. Harold Camping, *Open Forum* program, September 4, 1992.

25. Harold Camping, *1994?* (Vantage, 1992), xvi.

26. Mary Stewart Relfe, *Economic Advisor*, February 28, 1983.

27. Lester Sumrall, *I Predict 2000 AD* (South Bend, IN: Sumrall, 1987), 74.

28. Robert L. Reymond, *Jesus, Divine Messiah: The New Testament Witness* (Phillipsburg, NJ: Presbyterian & Reformed, 1990), 80.

29. Thomas Schultz, quoted in Josh McDowell and Bart Larson, *Jesus: A Biblical Defense of His Deity* (San Bernardino, CA: Here's Life, 1975), 54.

30. Robert Reymond, quoted in McDowell and Larson, *Jesus*, 54.

Chapter 7—The Second Coming of Jesus Christ

1. *The Bible Knowledge Commentary* (Wheaton, IL: Victor Publishers, 1983), The Bible Study App, Olive Tree Software.

2. *The HCSB Study Bible* (Nashville, TN: Holman Publishers, 2015), The Bible Study App, Olive Tree Software.

3. *The Moody Bible Commentary* (Chicago, IL: Moody, 2014), The Bible Study App, Olive Tree Software.

Chapter 8—The Judgment of the Nations and the Millennial Kingdom

1. Stanley Toussaint, *Behold the King: A Study of Matthew* (Grand Rapids, MI: Kregel, 2005), 291.

2. Merrill F. Unger, *Beyond the Crystal Ball* (Chicago, IL: Moody, 1978), 134-35.

3. J. Dwight Pentecost, *The Words and Works of Jesus Christ* (Grand Rapids, MI: Zondervan, 1978), 410; insert added for clarification. See also J. Dwight Pentecost, *Things to Come* (Grand Rapids, MI: Zondervan, 1978), 418.

4. *The Bible Knowledge Commentary*, New Testament, eds. Roy B. Zuck and John F. Walvoord (Wheaton, IL: Victor, 1983), 81.

5. John F. Walvoord, *Major Bible Prophecies* (Grand Rapids, MI: Zondervan, 1991), 390.

6. Charles C. Ryrie, *Biblical Theology of the New Testament* (Chicago, IL: Moody, 1979), 92.

7. Ryrie, *Biblical Theology*, 76.

8. Lewis Sperry Chafer, *Systematic Theology* (Dallas, TX: Dallas Seminary Press, 1948), 5:137.

9. Ryrie, *Biblical Theology*, 76.

10. See Charles L. Feinberg, "The Eternal Kingship of Christ," in *Jesus the King Is Coming* (Chicago, IL: Moody, 1975), 185.

11. See Toussaint, *Behold the King*, 289.

Chapter 9—The Intermediate State, Resurrections, and Judgments

1. Oswald Sanders, *Heaven: Better by Far* (Grand Rapids, MI: Discovery House, 1993), 91.

2. Wayne Grudem, *Systematic Theology: An Introduction to Biblical Doctrine* (Grand Rapids, MI: Zondervan, 1994), 831.

Chapter 10—The Eternal State

1. Warren W. Wiersbe, *The Bible Exposition Commentary*, 2:621, in The Bible Study App, Olive Tree Software.

Chapter 12—Lessons Learned from the Seven Churches, Part 2

1. Renald Showers, *Maranatha: Our Lord Come!* (Bellmawr, NJ: Friends of Israel, 1995), 214.

2. Arnold Fruchtenbaum, *The Footsteps of the Messiah*, Logos Bible Software.

Postscript: You Can Trust Biblical Prophecy

1. Norman Geisler and Ron Brooks, *When Skeptics Ask* (Wheaton, IL: Victor Books, 1990), 115.

2. John Ankerberg, John Weldon, and Walter C. Kaiser, *The Case for Jesus the Messiah* (Chattanooga, TN: The John Ankerberg Evangelistic Association, 1989), 16.